COLLEGE.EDU

■ ■

Online Resources for the
Cyber-Savvy Student

VERSION 8.0
LISA@LISAGUERNSEY.COM
(LISA GUERNSEY)

Address correspondence to:

Octameron Associates
PO Box 2748
Alexandria, VA 22301
703. 836. 5480 (voice)
703. 836. 5650 (fax)
www.octameron.com
info@octameron.com

ISBN 1-57509-098-8
PRINTED IN THE UNITED STATES OF AMERICA

Many thanks to my husband, Rob,
for his wired advice and unwavering support.

TABLE OF CONTENTS

PREFACE

■■■■■■■■■■■■■■■■

GETTING STARTED

Consider yourself among the lucky. As a college-bound student, you have entered the market at a time when the Internet is making the college search, the application process, and the financial-aid quest easier than ever before. The World Wide Web is stocked with free (and helpful) directories and news sources; electronic mail makes it easy to ask questions; and digitization is streamlining tasks and eliminating the need for mindless paper pushing.

But, as many frustrated people have already discovered, the Internet comes with a major caveat: While good stuff is out there, it can be a nightmare to find. No one wants to waste an afternoon clicking through pages of outdated drivel and useless promotions, attempting to download files that never seem to work, and waiting for oversized color advertisements to etch themselves across the screen.

This book will help you avoid that wasted time. It directs you to Web sites and online areas with useful information, instead of those that simply act as indices pointing you elsewhere. (Unless otherwise noted, sites appear in order of what I consider the most useful.)

- It provides WARNINGS about sites with heavy graphics and programs that require additional software and computer memory to run.

- It alerts you to pages you should save as BOOKMARKS or favorites.

- And it offers TIPS to make surfing the Internet, in general, more worth your while.

If this is your first time meandering through the Internet, take a few minutes to read Appendix 2: FAQs for Internet Newbies. It will help you get your bearings.

| Warnings | Bookmarks | Tips |

PART ONE
■■■■■■■■■■■■■■■■■■■
Getting Plugged In

CHAPTER 1

■■■■■■■■■■■■■■■■■■■

SITE SEEING: THE BASICS

Consider this the scaled-down, one-stop shop for college-bound students using the Internet. Use this 10-step program as a guide to essential links—or simply as a strategic outline to the chapters that follow.

Step One—Narrow your list of possible colleges.
nces.ed.gov/ipeds/cool/Search.asp
www.petersons.com
www.collegeboard.com
www.princetonreview.com

Step Two—Go to their home pages. Learn everything you can about the schools. Bookmark ones you like.
www.fastWeb.monster.com/fastsearch/college

Step Three—Collect objective news and information about the colleges.
www.newslink.org/news.html

Step Four—Take some virtual tours. E-mail questions along the way.
www.campustours.com
Or go to the home pages of the colleges you book-marked. (See Step Two)

Step Five—Meanwhile, prepare for the SAT or ACT.
icpac.indiana.edu/publications/infoseries/is-11.xml
www.collegeboard.com
www.act.org
www.testu.com

Step Six—Request, download, or bookmark applications for colleges that interest you.
Your best bet is to go to the colleges' home pages and head for the online admission office. (See Step Two.)

Step Seven—Complete your college applications— online if possible.
icpac.indiana.edu/publications/infoseries/is-15.xml
www.princetonreview.com/college/apply
www.applyweb.com

Step Eight—Collect financial-aid information, send in your FAFSA, and register for PROFILE (if necessary).
www.students.gov
www.fafsa.ed.gov
www.finaid.org
www.collegeboard.com

Step Nine—Conduct your own scholarship search.
www.fastWeb.monster.com
www.freschinfo.com

Step Ten—Hang out on the Internet instead of stressing out about acceptances.
www.collegeclub.com

CHAPTER 2

■■■■■■■■■■■■■■■■■■■■

CONNECTING AND COMMUNICATING

Connecting

So, how does the cyber-savvy student get started? The first step is to connect to the Internet using an online service or an Internet service provider.

Using online services

Online services provide subscribers with specialized content, as well as Internet access. Many people use America Online, by far the largest service. Or you might have an account with Microsoft Network(MSN), ATT.net or CompuServe—the latter is owned by AOL and focuses its services on a business audience.

Before you rev up one of these services, however, here are a few pointers:

- When you log in to an online service, you are connected to a large, international network—but you are not necessarily ON the Internet. You may be browsing through the specialized content made available to subscribers of that service only. AOL's College Prep area, for example, is open only to people on AOL.

- These services will give you direct access to the Web, however. To go directly to the Web, click on an area called "Search the Web" or something similar. Even if you do not go straight to the Web, you might find yourself clicking to a Web page without even realizing it. For example, links to Web pages are embedded throughout AOL. Once you are on these sites you have stepped out of the online service's closed territory and onto the Internet.

- The Internet's unlimited expanse can open up thousands of new sites for you to investigate. If you have a slow computer with a slow modem connection, however, you will sometimes receive information at a slower rate.

- America Online provides several areas for college-bound students and parents that are useful to click through. The service also links you to

Web sites, most of which are described and indexed in this book, and which may be worth more of your time than the content on AOL itself.

Using Internet-service providers

Internet-service providers, or ISPs, offer Internet connections for either an hourly or monthly fee. They do not provide content, but they let you go straight to your e-mail account or the Web by opening up a browser like Netscape or Internet Explorer (browsers are pieces of software that translate text code into splashy, colorful Web pages). Sometimes ISPs have "start pages" (the first screen you see when you log on) with links to popular Web sites and search engines, like Yahoo!. In your search for college admission information, most of your research will occur on the Web.

Earthlink, AT&T and Sprint have all become national ISPs. You'll find local ones listed at www.thelist.com.

Communicating

Once you successfully connect to an online service or an ISP, you'll be able to communicate with financial-aid and admission professionals, as well as other students across the world. You do this over the Internet using the World Wide Web, electronic mail, and Usenet.

Using the World Wide Web

Whether you connect to the Internet using an online service or an ISP, you'll find the Web can be slow—especially if you're trying to load a graphics-heavy site and you're using an old, slow modem. When you are looking for college-related information, you may not need to see all of those graphics and would rather receive the text only. You can make this happen by changing the way your browser loads images. (For more information, see the section titled "Why do some sites take so long to load? And what can I do about it?" in Appendix 2.)

If you have access to a computer at your school or library with a faster, more direct Internet connection, use it, especially if you'd like to take some of the graphics-heavy "virtual tours" found on many college home pages.

For more information on the differences between Dial-Up connections (like modems and ISDNs) and Dedicated Services (like DSL and Cable), see Apprendix 2.

Using e-mail

Even as snazzy graphics, jazzy sounds, and animated images flood the Internet, simple e-mail remains one of its prize attributes. It is quick, convenient, and accessible to folks all over the world, regardless of how advanced their computer systems are. Use it when you can—but be aware of the following as well:

- When you visit chat rooms and forums, you may unknowingly pass your e-mail address along to companies and individuals who will later send you junk messages you don't want. In fact, Web-based marketing companies are dying to find out your e-mail address. They want the chance to send you unsolicited advertisements, which can quickly clog your mail box. Be careful where you tread. Appendix 2 includes some tips to help reduce junk e-mail.

- Be polite and open in your e-mail messages—especially those you send to admission offices and alumni. Never send just a one-line question like, "Is this a good college?" You'll get no response and annoy the person on the other end. Instead, state your name and where you are from. Ask specific questions. And always say "thank you." It sounds obvious, but it's amazing how many people abandon good manners when shielded by the anonymity of the Internet.

Using Usenet newsgroups

Usenet (short for "User's Network") represents an older part of the Internet; it's essentially a network of tens of thousands of bulletin boards, or newsgroups, arranged by subject matter.

Before the Web became the dominant force of the Internet, these newsgroups were only available to people with "newsreading" or "newsserver" programs, for example, NN Newsreaders (for UNIX machines), and uAccess (for Macintosh machines). Computers in many universities and public libraries still use some sort of newsreader software.

Hooking up with a newsgroup is getting easier. If you plan to track a newsgroup over time, you should "subscribe" using your Web browser or online service. For example:

- If you are an AOL user, go to keyword "newsgroups" and select the icon titled "expert add." From there you can simply type in the name of the newsgroup you want. Clicking "Add newsgroups" enables you to browse through lists of newsgroups before determining exactly which one you want to add.

- If you are using Netscape, that means clicking on "mail and newsgroups" (under "Window") in the file menu. A new window will open. Click on "subscribe" and put a check next to the newsgroups you wish to add.

• And if you are using Microsoft's Internet Explorer, go to "Read News" under "Mail and News" in the Tools menu. Depending on how your Internet service is set up, you may have to update "properties," including the name of your news (NNTP) server. If you don't know (who would?) check with your ISP.

Most newsgroups focus on a single topic, and it's hard to think of something that's not yet covered. (There's even one dedicated to dining hall food.) Once you add a newsgroup, your browser will show you that link every time you switch to your newsgroup list.

If you decide to subscribe to a newsgroup, and be an active participant (rather than a "lurker"), look through the posted messages for a link to that group's "FAQs" (Frequently Asked Questions). Most newsgroups have their own do's and don'ts, and their members have cruel things to say to rule-breakers.

Even if you don't have easy access to newsgroups, you can still check them for relevant information—Google Groups provides web-based access to all messages posted to Usenet since 1981, archiving 845 million messages from more than 50,000 discussion groups. The Google folks update this archive several times each day; you can search it from their home page at groups.google.com. (Note: This archive was previously maintained by DejaNews, and acquired by Google a few years ago.)

In searching for reliable information about colleges, financial aid, and other topics, don't waste too much time trying to learn newsgroup software or wading through groups on the Web. The newsgroup arena is massive—and hunting for good information is like searching for a needle in a haystack. If you have a specific question, however, feel free to post it to the appropriate newsgroup. You never know what sort of valuable information someone might post in response.

Using mailing lists

You can also have financial-aid and admission information delivered straight to your e-mail inbox by subscribing to mailing lists. Currently, many lists relating to college are designed for admission and financial-aid professionals, and the information can be quite technical. Also, sponsoring organizations often restrict their lists to members-only. But keep your eyes open—some companies will offer to keep you posted about changes or additions to their site. Subscribe, and you'll be spared the trouble of constantly rechecking for new material.

One Last Word of Advice

In the razzle-dazzle and convenience of the Internet, don't forget the real world. Talk to the people around you—your parents, friends, siblings, and counselors—about their own experiences in selecting and applying to colleges. Stop by your public library—it's stocked with books that might answer questions the Internet cannot. And visit colleges in person. Nothing beats the experience of physically walking on a campus and talking to the students.

PART TWO

■■■■■■■■■■■■■■■■■■■■■■

Search, Snoop and Select

CHAPTER 3

■■■■■■■■■■■■■■■■■■■

SEARCHING ONLINE DATABASES

How can the Internet help you find the perfect college? First, search a variety of online databases to find colleges that fit your interests and visit their home pages to get more detailed information. Next, snoop through college newspapers, and take some virtual tours. Last, select your final choices by gathering impartial information and conducting some interviews of your own.

Collecting Information About Colleges

The Internet isn't perfect, but one of its major strengths is the ease with which you can search through its vast network of information. Finding a college that meets your criteria is suddenly much easier than poring over a 300-page printed directory. Just enter what you want—a small college on the West Coast with an ecology major; a public university with good wheelchair access; or a New England school with study-abroad programs. Then click, and watch the Internet churn out lists of colleges that match.

Several companies design huge Web sites to accommodate this kind of searching. They hope to draw crowds so they can attract advertisers. I call these areas "metasites." In addition to search capabilities, they try to do everything else, too. Some provide how-to articles on getting into college, discussion areas for questions about college essays or campus tours, and financial-aid tips. In most cases, their search engines are their most useful attribute, but they are worth exploring for other information, too.

For a full list of metasites, see Appendix 1. For tips on getting better search results, see Appendix 2.

COOL's Web search

nces.ed.gov/ipeds/cool/Search.asp

There are three good reasons to visit this site, which is part of a new program called College Opportunities Online (COOL). First, it is administered by the National Center for Education Statistics, the federal government's primary agency for collecting current educational data. Second, you can use the search engine without having to register, or reveal any personal data. And third, it allows you to search by geographic region right away, instead of having to select specific states. Once you've selected the criteria that matter most, the matching colleges will appear on your screen. You can then click on the school name to see tuition rates for the past three years. Other useful statistics include average aid awards (including the source of funds), and enrollment numbers by ethnicity, gender, and the types of degrees conferred.

Peterson's College Search

www.petersons.com

Click on "Two and Four Year Colleges" under "Education Search" to search through a database that, according to Peterson's, includes every accredited college in the United States and many in Canada. The "Detailed Search" section lets you find colleges by location, majors offered, tuition, enrollment size, religious affiliation, or selectivity; or simply look up a college by typing in its name.

After you've received a list of colleges that meet your criteria, you can scan some quick facts about the college, compare it to others you've selected, go to the college's Web site, add information about the college to your personal organizer, or send the college an instant inquiry requesting a catalog, application, or financial aid information. In many cases, you can also click on "Apply" and start filling out the college's application right away. (For more information about online applications, see Chapter 8.)

Like most college search sites, you will need to register with your name, address and email before you can take advantage of all the site's features.

Sometimes you will be faced with a list of things—like states or college names—in a scrolling window on a Web page. To select more than one listing at a time, hold down the Control or Command button on your keyboard when you click on the multiple items you want to include in your search.

College Board Search

www.collegeboard.com

From the College Board's main page, use "College Quick Finder" to search the College Board's 3,500-school database simply by typing in a college's name. If you're not ready for such specifics, click on "Advanced College Search" to complete a mini-questionnaires about the type of school and campus setting you want. For example, if you search by type of school, you'll get to a page asking whether you seek a private or public college, a single-sex or co-ed college, a large or small college, a historically black college, and/or a college affiliated with a specific religion. The resulting list will tell you about admission requirements, tuition costs, student life, degrees offered and much more.

If you have already found a school that meets your basic requirements, you can use the College Board's "Like Find" feature to locate additional colleges with similar features—an easy way to expand your pool of possible colleges.

The Princeton Review's Counselor-O-Matic

www.princetonreview.com/college/research

Counselor-O-Matic (from The Princeton Review) asks you about your courses, grades, test scores and extracurriculars, as well as your college preferences—location, size, setting, academics, selectivity, cost, student life, and sports. What's different is that you get to weigh the importance of many of these preferences.

Counselor-O-Matic then matches you up with a selection of schools that might be right for you, divided into three categories—Good Matches, Reaches and Safeties. (The site says, "no promises" and reminds students of the vagaries of the admission process, but it's a painless way to get an early read on your chances.) From this "Results" page, you can go to a school's Web site or view detailed information about the college, such as its faculty-to-student ratio or how it handles advanced placement tests. If you want to register, you can also use the service's online applications and send inquiries to request more information.

Many Web sites ask you to register to use their free services. Behind the scenes, these registrations are bartering chips, enabling the site's developers to prove to advertisers that the sites has a young, marketable audience. But beware: when you register by typing in your e-mail name and address, you are giving up some of your online privacy. Depending on the company's privacy policy, advertisers will often use that information to find you. You can avoid some of the hassle by keeping your eyes open for registration checkboxes that say things like, "Yes, I would love to receive e-mail messages about new products." If, in fact, you have no desire to receive these veiled advertisements, make sure that the check box is not marked in any way that would imply your permission.

XAP's Mentor Web Sites

www.xap.com/gotocollege

Use XAP's "College Finder" or "College Matching Wizard" to narrow your search. The interface is clean and friendly.

XAP has also created "Mentor Systems" for over 25 states, including CT Mentor, IllinoisMentor, TexasMentor, NYMentor, and GeorgiaMentor. At most of these sites, students can use the "Matching Assistant" to find and rank the best school for them, as well as take virtual campus tours, apply for admission online, and learn about financial aid opportunities. You can link directly to these sites from within XAP. XAP has recently added two additional mentor systems—Christian College Mentor and HBCU Mentor, a guide to Historically Black Colleges and Universities.

You might want to skip questions about the level of tuition your family is willing (or able) to pay so as not to limit your search unnecessarily. Remember, more expensive colleges often award more generous aid packages, so a $20,000 college may cost you no more out-of-pocket than a $10,000 college.

Best College Picks, From Peterson's

www.bestcollegepicks.com

This new tool from Peterson's asks you a series of questions about your abilities, goals and values, then develops a personal profile based on your responses and matches your profile to a list of possible colleges. The results are fun, and interesting, but should be used only in conjunction with other search methods. When we asked a group of college graduates to take the quiz, we were surprised that none of them were matched to their alma maters, especially since they all enjoyed their college experience.

Colleges Want You!, From Peterson's

www.collegeswantyou.com

This search option from Peterson's lets colleges find you. You simply enter your background data—personal, as well as academic. Colleges can then access your profile, and if there is a match, Peterson's will provide the interested school with your contact information (name, street address, and e-mail address).

CollegeNET
cnsearch.collegenet.com

Search through more than 4,000 colleges based on tuition cost, enrollment type (public, private, or religious affiliation), majors, and intercollegiate sports. CollegeNET retrieves matching colleges quickly—displayed in alphabetical order, but sortable by tuition rate, test scores, enrollment size, ethnicity, or application deadline. By clicking on a college's name, you'll get additional information including a link to the college's home page, an online application, tuition data and details about admissions, financial aid, campus life and academics. CollegeNET also searches databases of information about MBA Programs, vocational/technical schools, and medical or nursing schools.

Find Your Ideal School, by *U.S. News*
www.usnews.com/usnews/edu/college/tools/brief/cosearch_brief.php

Search the magazine's online directory of 1,400 colleges by name. For advanced search options like how far away from home you want to be, how much you can afford, selectivity, academic programs and varsity sports programs, use the magazine's Advanced College Search." To do so, though, you must subscribe to *US News'* Premium Online Edition (for $12.95).

Some searchable databases may look complete—even when they are vastly understocked. Some sites only provide information on colleges they have under contract or colleges listed in specific directories. Don't be fooled into thinking these are the only colleges that exist. And never rely on just one database, unless you can be sure the information is comprehensive.

Your best bet may be the federal government's searchable data base (COOL), run by the National Center for Education Statistics and mentioned at the beginning of this chapter. It includes 9,000 institutions of higher education in the United States.

CollegeXpress
www.collegexpress.com

A snazzy look at nearly 700 "featured" private colleges (and a few public ones), based on profiles provided by the colleges themselves. In addition, you'll find "Vital Information" on nearly 3,000 two- and four-year colleges. Produced by the publishers of *Private Colleges & Universities* magazine.

The College Guide

www.mycollegeguide.org

Search by region, cost, freshman-class size, surrounding community size, or school type.

CollegeView

www.collegeview.com/collegesearch/index.epl

CollegeView lets you search over 3,800 college profiles by area of study, location, student-body size, religious affiliation, athletic programs, on-campus activities, financial aid, city size, special programs and services for the disabled. You'll receive detailed results for each college—including data on international student and minority student representation. CollegeView also links you to multimedia virtual tours (for its featured schools), complete with audio clips and home page links.

> When typing addresses, or URLs, into a Web browser, type exactly what you see—even if it seems something's missing. Some addresses, for example, end in ".htm" and others end in "html". The files with ".htm" endings were probably created on computers that did not allow four-character file extensions. Web browsers read ".htm" files without a problem—but if you type ".html" on a file named ".htm," the browser may give you an error message.

Looking for Specific Types of Schools

If you want to cut to the chase and search only for information on historically black colleges or Catholic colleges for example, these sites might help. The next section of this chapter, "Finding and using college home pages," offers some options, too.

HBCU Central

www.hbcu-central.com

This nicely revamped site provides a gateway to the HBCU Web—a list of home pages for Historically Black Colleges and Universities—as well as a guide to what issues are facing HBCUs. Includes information and links to government programs and initiatives, electronic newspapers, online journals and information networks for the African-American community.

Hillel

www.hillel.org

Hillel, the national organization of Jewish college students, has put together a sharp Web site on student life. Click on "Guide to Jewish Life on Campus" and you'll find links to Hillel chapters at over 500 colleges throughout the world. Learn whether a college provides kosher meals, how many Jewish students are on campus, whether religious services are held on-or off-campus, how many Jewish Studies courses the school offers, whether the school has a "Study in Israel" program, and how active the Jewish student population is.

The Association of Jesuit Colleges and Universities

www.ajcunet.edu

Nationwide, there are 28 Jesuit Colleges—from Boston College in Massachusetts to Xavier University in Ohio. Use the site's U.S. map to find one near you, or use the site's search service to seek out the college that offers the major you like in the location you want.

Studyabroad.com

www.studyabroad.com

If spending a semester abroad is important to you, do some research on which programs are available through which universities before you apply. This directory will let you search programs in more than 100 countries, and link you to the sponsoring school's home page for more information.

Collegeabroad.com

www.collegeabroad.com

If you'd rather spend all four years abroad, and earn your degree from an international college or university, you can start your research here. Like its sister-site above, Collegeabroad.com lets you search through full-degree programs worldwide and links you to the sponsoring school's home page for more information.

Finding and Using College Home Pages

Most colleges have pumped up their Web sites—or home pages—as a way to recruit new students. So be sure to go to the Web pages of colleges that interest you. You'll often find:

- Maps and parking information—print these out before you leave for a campus tour.

- Admission information, including applications to download or complete on line—check deadlines and requirements before you apply.
- Calendars of special events and academic schedules—get a sense of what is offered year-round.
- Press releases—take a peek at the administration's view on what's happened lately, or find out which faculty members are in the news.
- Electronic viewbooks—take a cyber-peek around the college, remembering that professional photographers and copywriters are paid lots of money to make it look and sound good.
- Financial-aid information—find out about special scholarships, payment plans, and application deadlines.
- Student-activity links—get more information on sports and clubs of interest, student services, even the career center's resources.
- Directories—link up with current students, staff, faculty, and alumni. You'll find e-mail addresses and personal home pages.
- Links to student newspapers—read students' views on news, academics, and social life.
- Statistics and data—look up graduation rates, sizes of entering classes, and faculty-to-student ratios.
- Invitations to online open houses—meet prospective students in real time over the Net.
- Did I mention the library? Often, you can browse the cyber-stacks.

What you should not do, however, is use these home pages as your sole source of information. Consider much of what you see as a digital brochure. Each college will put itself in the best possible light, hiding all flaws as best it can. Don't be swayed by a sunny photograph of the library when you have yet to see the rest of the campus. On the other hand, don't write off a college just because it doesn't have a snazzy Web site.

The following sites will link you to college home pages. They are listed in order of increasing specificity.

fastSEARCH
www.fastWeb.monster.com/fastsearch/college

The makers of FastWeb, an online scholarship database, have opened a useful directory of colleges' home pages—including links that take you straight to a school's admission application and its financial aid and admission pages. Organized by state and school name.

YAHOO!'s College Listings

dir.yahoo.com/Education/Higher_Education/
Colleges_and_Universities

Yahoo! includes one of the most complete lists of college home pages—including universities around the world. From the link above, you'll get to a page that offers you the option of searching "By Region." Click that to get to home pages for universities in the United States, organized alphabetically by state, or to schools in other countries, organized by country.

U.S. Universities and Community Colleges

www.utexas.edu/world/univ

The folks at the University of Texas at Austin regularly update this comprehensive index. It provides links to home pages organized alphabetically or by state. It's an easy, no-frills way to get to the Web pages for your preferred colleges.

All About College—Search Internationally

www.allaboutcollege.com

This site provides a comprehensive directory of universities around the world. Click on "College Directory," then choose a region in which you'd like to study, and you'll be linked to home pages of that country's schools. The listings for schools in the United States include e-mail addresses for admission offices.

Independent Higher Education Network

www.fihe.org/tools/map.asp

Search tips as well as links to nearly all private universities in the United States, and to organizations in each state that act as advocacy groups for private colleges.

Canadian Colleges

www.uwaterloo.ca/canu/index.html

Links to all institutional members of the Association of Universities and Colleges of Canada as well as related sites on studying in Canada.

The Women's College Coalition

www.womenscolleges.org

Links to women's colleges, as well as a history of women's colleges, lists of notable graduates and a calendar of events at women's colleges.

Community College Web

www.mcli.dist.maricopa.edu/cc

Links to more than 1,250 community colleges in the United States and nearly 200 resources related to community colleges.

Community College Finder

www.aacc.nche.edu

The American Association of Community Colleges site links you to member institutions and provides statistics, history factoids, lists of outstanding community-college alumni, and a report on the fastest-growing occupations.

Professional and Graduate Schools

www.gradschools.com/search.html

A fairly comprehensive list of graduate school programs—including everything from the basics (like business and law) to more obscure programs (like acupuncture and packaging science). You'll be led to general information about specific universities, as well as links to their home pages and e-mail addresses for their admission offices.

American Indian Higher Education Consortium

www.aihec.org

Provides an overview of tribal colleges and links to their home pages, plus a clickable map showing where all 35 are located. For colleges without Web sites, the site offers other contact information.

Hispanic Association of Colleges and Universities

www.hacu.net

Gateway to over 190 Hispanic-Serving Institutions (HSIs) located in eleven states and Puerto Rico as well as 105 Associate Members located in eighteen states. To be considered an HSI, 25% of the total enrollment must be Hispanic; for Associate Members, 10% of the total enrollment must be Hispanic. The site also describes a variety of student internships and provides links to numerous scholarship resources.

CHAPTER 4

■■■■■■■■■■■■■■■■■■■

SNOOPING FOR
THE REAL STORY

Reading College Newspapers

Browsing through student newspapers and other online news services is a good way to get a relatively objective view of a college. So snoop around. Is your number-one pick cutting services or raising tuition? Is your state's university opening a new dining hall, computer lab, or football stadium any time soon? Will the campus become a major construction zone for the first three years you are attending?

Before the Internet, these news developments were not always easy to discover—especially if you had not yet visited the campus. But student newspapers have leapt onto the Internet en masse—and many provide archives of back issues, allowing you to gain a better sense of what has been happening on campus all year.

U-WIRE
www.uwire.com

Read stories and headlines from hundreds of online student papers across the country. Created by journalism students at Northwestern University and now owned by a Web-based company called Student Advantage.

College News Online
www.collegenews.com

Includes a small but interesting collection of headlines from student newspapers across the country, in addition to fledgling job-search services.

If you already know which colleges you are interested in, you might have the most luck going straight to the college's home page and clicking to the student newspaper. Some colleges make it easy—they link to publications or news straight from their main page. Most of the time, though, you may have to poke around first. Try clicking on sections called "Student Life" or "Student Organizations" or search for the words "student newspaper." Or go to the directories of college papers listed on these pages.

News Link
newslink.org/statcamp.html

This is a great resource for news publications of any kind—including campus newspapers which are listed here alphabetically by state. Of course, you might find extra nuggets of information by searching through the professional newspapers that cover colleges you are considering. This site provides links to those papers as well, also organized by state.

Most college papers publish only sporadically during the summer, so take time during the school year to browse the online papers of colleges that interest you. To find interesting articles, try searching on words like tuition, arrests, construction, dining, protests.

The Chronicle of Higher Education
chronicle.com

If your parents work in education, they might have a subscription to *The Chronicle*. If so, tell them to bookmark this site and get a password (it's free to subscribers—just send an e-request to member-today@chronicle.com). Then you'll be able to plug into daily news on anything that affects colleges and universities. Your high school guidance counselor might have access, as well. Or, you can subscribe yourself for $7.25 per month.

But even if you don't have a subscription and password, you should browse the front page of the site where you can read headlines for the latest news affecting higher-education.

Getting the Regional Scoop

Check out these sites for details on colleges in the area of the country you'd like to make your next home. They are listed alphabetically.

Houston Area Higher Education Resources

www.chron.com/content/community/higher_ed/index.html

The Houston Chronicle's directory of college Web sites in the area, plus links to alumni associations, student organizations, student publications and more.

The New York Times' Education Coverage

www.nytimes.com/pages/education

Serves up daily news about education issues and events, including higher-education coverage—although there doesn't appear to be an online area that focuses on the college search. Check in on the education forums and don't miss the education-and-technology columns also available on line.

Southern California Schools and Colleges

www.latimes.com/news/learning

Updated daily, this section fills you in on the latest education news to hit the Los Angeles area and beyond. Sponsored by *The Los Angeles Times*.

The Washington CollegePost

washingtonpost.com/wp-dyn/education/highereducation

Read national news about trends in higher education, converse with college officials in online chats, and find directories to college home pages. Maintained by *The Washington Post*.

If the region you want is not listed here, go to the area's online newspaper and search using the keywords "college" or "higher education." Or click on the "community" sections to see if they have recent news on local colleges. To find the area's online newspaper, go to Newslink at newslink.org.

Thinking About Safety

Security on Campus, Inc.
www.campussafety.org

The mission of Security on Campus, Inc. is to prevent campus crime and violence. This site includes links to campus crime statistics, and information about legal rights and victim assistance programs—important background for all college-bound students.

What About College Rankings?

Colleges are virtually impossible to rank. There are so many variables— location, mission, size, tuition costs, professor-to-student ratios, you name it. College-bound students should never rely on simple numbered lists to find what they want. But despite the shallowness that results from rankings, various media outlets continue to promote them. Top-10 lists sell, after all. The following publications put their rankings on the Web.

U.S. News & World Report
www.usnews.com/usnews/edu/college/cohome.htm

Updated each August, U.S. News & World Report produces some of the most popular and influential lists—even though they are criticized by college officials throughout the country for turning college comparisons into a popularity contest. Take its ratings with a grain of salt. The site is well-designed, however, and full of other useful data, including a couple of less-controversial lists, such as rankings of colleges that have the most students receiving merit-based aid, the most students studying abroad, the most students in fraternities or sororities, or the most students over age 25.

The Princeton Review's Best 351 Colleges
www.princetonreview.com/college/research

Students are the experts here, ranking the country's "Best 351 Colleges." In publishing the survey results, The Princeton Review groups colleges by their top scores in academics, administration, quality of life, politics, demographics, social life, extracurriculars, and parties. This year's best school for overall academic experience? Yale University. What about the best parties? Top mentions go to University of Colorado-Boulder and University of Wisconsin-Madison.

You can also do a "reverse" search—enter a school's name and see whether students value it for a well-stocked library or a well-stocked bar.

Maclean's University Rankings

www.macleans.ca

Visit this site to learn how Maclean's Magazine ranks nearly 50 Canadian colleges. You'll find interesting articles, too. The rankings are posted each November.

Laissez-Faire Rankings

collegeadmissions.tripod.com

If you believe that quality and selectivity are one in the same, you might look here. The creator of this site argues that "college is 'chosen company' and attempts to rank colleges by the (quality of the) membership they attract." To develop this selectivity ranking, he looks at the school's number of applicants, percent accepted, percent yield, percent of students in the top tenth of their high school class, percent of students scoring well on the SAT, percent of students selected as National Merit Scholars, and percent of freshmen returning as sophomores.

College Ranking Service

www.rankyourcollege.com

This site takes a totally tongue-in-cheek approach to college rankings.

Thinking Critically

A few companies and colleges have sworn against rankings like those compiled by *U.S. News.* They have created sites and written online essays to describe their reasons, and they strive to provide what they say is a better service.

College and University Rankings

www.library.uiuc.edu/edx/rankings.htm

Librarians at the University of Illinois at Urbana-Champaign have put together a comprehensive site about college rankings—including references to articles about their validity. See their section on the controversy over rankings for a quick overview on how universities and associations are trying to fight ranking outfits like *U.S. News.*

You'll also find links to several more interesting rankings, like the Mother Jones list of Top Ten Activist Schools, the John Templeton Foundation list of Colleges that Encourage Character Development, and the Campus Squirrel Listings, which equate the quality of a university with the health of its overall squirrel population.

Online Guide to Evaluating Information Technology on Campus
www.educause.edu/consumerguide

A nonprofit group is now offering an online consumer guide to help students and parents determine what technology matters most on campus. Learn what questions to ask, such as "What percentage of students on this campus has full-time use of personal computers?" and "What library resources are available online?"

CHAPTER 5

■■■■■■■■■■■■■■■■■■■

SELECTING THE BEST
SCHOOLS FOR YOU

Decisions. Decisions. You've seen what's out there, and it's almost more than you can take. You should apply to no more than six colleges; so how will you decide which would be best? First, take some campus tours…in person, if possible. Otherwise, explore the virtual world. Next, gather as much additional advice as you can—from college experts as well as your peers. And finally, do some interviews of your own.

Preparing For a Campus Tour—The Real Thing

The best way to learn about a college is to visit in person, talk to real students, stay in real dorms, sit in on real classes, and eat real dining-hall food. But don't you dare arrive on a campus blind, driving around end-lessly looking for parking only to find that the college doesn't give tours on the day you've arrived. You have no excuse now that the Internet exists. Before you take off for a trip, do five things:

1) Read the College Board's collection of articles on planning college visits (www.collegeboard.com/csearch/college_visits). Figure out the best time for you to make your visits, as well as what kind of campus setting you enjoy most—the big city, the 'burbs or the wilds.

2) Go to the home page of the college you are planning to visit. You will probably find those necessary details, such as the hours of operation for the admissions office, the location of the undergraduate library, and how to get to the visitors' parking lot. If you'd like to sit in on a class, browse the course catalog. Jot down classroom numbers and times. Also, take a look at the college's calendar of events. You might want to plan your trip around the Asian-American Student Association's annual bash, or the next home soccer game.

3) At the admissions page, find out whether the college requires on-campus interviews. If you can't tell from the information supplied, look for an

admission office e-mail address and send a message asking what is recommended. (See Chapter 9's section on interviews for more information.)

4) Then go to CitySearch (www.citysearch.com) or Digital City (www.digitalcity.com) and search using the name of the town you are visiting. If it is a relatively large town, you'll probably at least find a map of the area and a restaurant guide. You might even find a service that gives you hotel rates and tourism tips. After all, if your parents (and/or siblings) plan to join you, you might as well turn the college tour into this year's family vacation.

5) If you're driving, use MapQuest (www.MapQuest.com) to plan your journey. Plug in your home address and your final destination and you'll get door-to-door directions, as well as detailed maps showing each and every turn on the way.

Taking a Campus Tour—Virtually

These just aren't the same as the real thing. No one disputes that. But taking virtual tours—which are usually similar to watching videos or slow slide shows—can give you a better sense of a campus than staring at a static brochure. If a college offers a virtual tour, it will usually link you to its "campus tour" from the front page or its admission section.

But before you take the plunge, take note:

1) Tours that describe themselves as videos usually require utilities known as "plug-ins," like QuickTime or RealVideo. If you have not updated your Web browsing software — like Internet Explorer or Netscape — in several years, you may have to download and install these plug-ins before the tours will work. (For more information, see Appendix 2.)

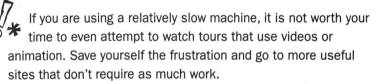 If you are using a relatively slow machine, it is not worth your time to even attempt to watch tours that use videos or animation. Save yourself the frustration and go to more useful sites that don't require as much work.

2) Don't take these tours during the Internet's rush hour. Avoid the early evening, when millions of people are taking a look online. Try them in the early morning or late at night to avoid slow-downs. These tours are built around color photographs, which can take longer than other files to appear on your browser.

3) Be prepared to get "stuck" in a virtual tour: You have clicked on the arrows, seen a few photos, and have had your fill. How do you find your

way back? If you're using a fairly advanced browser, you should be able to pull down a menu of sites you've visited by dragging on the space where you key in the URL. From there you can select the address you'd like to revisit. If you can't find it, hit the "back" button until you find your way out.

CampusTours.com
www.campustours.com

For a direct route to a college's virtual tour, head to this index. Colleges are listed by state, and alphabetically. Virtual tours offer 360 degree views of everything from student centers to athletic facilities to dorm rooms.

More entertaining, however, are college cams. Web cameras, called cams for short, have been installed on campuses around the country, and they are taking snapshots of sidewalk scenes, dorm rooms and student buildings every few moments. Those minute-by-minute photographs can be viewed on the Web, and this site will lead you straight to them.

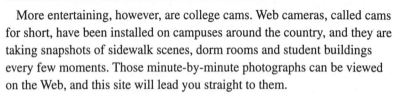

Some of these tours have words like (975K gif) in parentheses next to the links. Pay attention to this information if your computer is slow or old. A GIF is an acronym for a graphic that shows up on the Web. It is derived from the file extension ".gif" (graphics interchange format) that tells the computer the file is a type of compressed image. Another type of graphic is called JPEG (Joint Photographic Experts Group). In general, 975K is a whopping file, while 9K is something every computer should be able to handle quickly.

CollegeView's Virtual Tours
www.collegeview.com

Click on "Campus Tour" under "CollegeView Features" for a list of e-destinations. The multimedia presentations include audio clips.

Collegiate Choice Walking Tours Videos
www.collegiatechoice.com

A catalog of in-depth videos based on more than 350 college campuses, conducted candidly and independently of the colleges themselves. Some videos run for more than an hour, presenting interviews with students on campus and video clips from the college's walking tours. The cost is $15 per video, with $8 per order more for shipping.

Gathering More Advice

If you're not already overwhelmed with advice from your folks, your high-school guidance counselor, your friends, and random junk mail, you might want to take a peek on line. You'll find chat rooms where you can question "experts," forums where you can read people's posts and add your own, plus general advice and time-management tips.

The College Board's Starting Points for Parents and Students
www.collegeboard.com

Within its sections on "Plan for College" and "College Search," the College Board offers several useful clusters of essays, including "High School Steps" and "Tips For Finding Your College Match."

About.Com's College Admission Section
collegeapps.about.com

Read essays full of worthwhile advice, and check the college admissions chats and forums. About.com also takes you to dozens of other college planning sites, many of which are listed in this book.

U.S. News's College Forums
www.usnews.com/usnews/edu/forums/fohome.htm

Click on the "College" forum and you'll find dozens of questions from confused students just like you. U.S. News has pulled together a panel of admission and financial-aid experts to answer your most vexing questions.

Bolt
www.bolt.com

Bolt is aimed at 15- to 24-year-olds, a place where young adults can speak their minds on whatever subject they choose. Under "Boards" go to "College" and choose from a variety of topics.

College Comparison Worksheet
www.usnews.com/usnews/edu/college/cohome.htm

Are you still trying to narrow your options? Are there three or four colleges you simply can't choose between? Premium Subscribers to the *U.S. News* site may use this online worksheet to analyze how they differ. It might be smart, however, to apply to several of them anyway—just in case you don't get into the one you thought was a perfect fit.

Petersons (www.petersons.com) and The College Board (www.collegeboard.com) feature free side-by-side college comparisons, however, these sites display considerably less data in their comparisons.

College Personality Quiz

www.usnews.com/usnews/edu/college/tools/cpq/coquiz.htm

If you need to re-examine what you're looking for in a school, you might take the (free) *U.S. News* "College Personality Quiz."

If you come across a site that charges a fee to help you get into school, it is probably not worth the money. Some, in fact, are true scams. With all the free information available—and easily accessible on the Internet—there is little need for such services. Besides, 80% of all students get into their first-choice school; 95% get into one of their top two choices. What about that other 5%? They probably didn't do their webwork, so they applied to colleges that weren't right for them in the first place!

Dear Admissions Guru . . .

www.mycollegeguide.org/guru

Here you'll find answers to college planning questions provided by a well-meaning Web personality named the Admissions Guru.

Getting Ready for University

www.campusaccess.com

Although it is aimed at students planning to go to Canadian schools, the "education" section of this site can help students anywhere decide whether to stay close to home or move far away, or whether to choose a small town or head to a larger city. It also includes essays on saying goodbye to high school and getting ready for college.

For more Web sites that offer general advice, see the "metasites" listed in Appendix 1.

The Princeton Review's Forums

discuss.princetonreview.com

Jump into discussions with other students about choosing a college, the latest movies, college life, help with your high school homework, and nearly everything else. First, you'll have to register. There's also an "advice" section to help you through the selection process as well as guidance tools for counselors and parents.

Using Newsgroups

Soc.college.admissions

Browsing newsgroups can be very hit-or-miss. Many contain little useful information and loads of cheap advertisements and ugly language. The soc.college.admissions group, however, is one of the better ones. At last check, for example, one thread was on which schools are "Ivy equivalent."

Hooking up with a newsgroup is getting easier. If you plan to track a newsgroup over time, you can easily "subscribe" using your Web browser or online service. Or you can get there by going to groups.google.com. For more information, review the section on "Using Usenet Newsgroups" in Chapter 2.

Soc.college

This newsgroup usually contains more garbage than valuable information. But once in a while, someone will post a question asking about something like the differences between two colleges or the social life on a campus. You might have the most luck if you post your own specific question and check back a week later to find out whether anyone has offered any intelligent answers to it.

Don't get sucked in. You can waste hours clicking around newsgroups searching for a gem of information, hogging the phone line all afternoon. Meanwhile, you could be exploring useful Web sites.

Do Some Interviews of Your Own

Finally, and most importantly, don't be afraid to do your own interviewing. In this era of hyper-communication, you have the tools at hand to find professors and students who might be able to answer specific questions. Some admissions offices will provide names of students whom you may contact through e-mail. Give them a try. But you might get a more balanced sense of what people truly think about the college by contacting the students in various organizations or professors in various departments.

How do you find them? First, go to the college's home page. Then, instead of clicking on the admission office link, click on one for "Student Life," "Student Organizations," or something similar. Browse around depending on your interests. Some student unions have developed fairly sophisticated Web pages, which include student e-mail addresses. Send e-mail straight from the Web if you are on your own computer, or jot down their addresses to use later.

The same strategy will work for professors. If you click on a section with a title like "Academic Departments," or "College of Arts and Sciences," you'll eventually come to a list of department pages. Click on those that interest you, and find addresses for professors.

> Sending e-mail, especially to professors, does not guarantee a response. They may not have time to respond to queries from students they do not know (or who aren't in one of their classes). You will get the best results if you send personal and targeted e-mail messages with very specific questions.

Don't forget alumni networks, either. Some universities link straight to an alumni section from their home pages. You might get lucky and find some e-mail addresses for recent alums there. Don't hesitate to drop them a note.

World Alumni Net

www.Alumni.net

This site gives you direct access to alums from high school and college who have volunteered their e-mail and home page addresses. Search by state, by school, and by year of graduation.

> Use e-mail etiquette when sending notes to enrolled students and professors. Always state clearly why you are writing, and ask specific, thoughtful questions. Lastly, always sign your name, your e-mail address, and hometown or high school at the bottom of the message. You never know if these are professors or students you will someday meet in class—so make a good impression!

The Daily Jolt
www.dailyjolt.com

A collection of (unofficial) college web sites created and run by students who actually attend the college. You can get a nice sense of each included school through listings of on- and off-campus events, daily Dining Hall menus, dorm room tours, ride boards, course catalogues, course evaluations, and more. You can also interact with students at the schools through discussion forums and links to student home pages.

 To get a full sense of a college, don't limit your "conversations" to a single student or alum. And never let one strange home page color your impression of an entire school.

CHAPTER 6

■■■■■■■■■■■■■■■■■■■■■■

CONSIDERING DISTANCE EDUCATION
AND COOPERATIVE EDUCATION

Today's collegiate environment is changing fast, so even if you're short on cash, short on time, or older than traditional college students, you can still earn a college degree. The two most popular alternatives to the typical four-year degree are distance education and cooperative education.

Learning About Distance Education

Distance education has become a hot—and hyped—discussion topic in education circles today. Even the most traditional institutions have pulled their heads out of the sand to get involved. If you are looking for a traditional, on-campus experience, chances are the college you select will be offering some online education as well.

If you are looking for a less-traditional experience, you'll have more choices than ever. Single and/or working parents are some of the most common enrollees of Internet-based college programs. Students with disabilities, especially, may find distance education an attractive alternative option. But remember these two caveats:

First, work smart. Online courses number in the thousands, so make certain you select ones that will earn you credits toward a recognized degree.

Second, be careful. The concept of Internet-based education is still so new it can be difficult to sort out the legitimate, worthwhile programs from the rip-offs. For starters, check to see if a program is accredited by a nationally recognized agency or if it has a relationship with other accredited colleges. Some bricks and mortar colleges find a combination of on-site courses and off-site Net-based courses work best.

Accreditation

Accreditation is like a stamp of approval—awarded only to educational programs that meet specific standards of quality. Future employers, for example, will need reassurance that you graduated from a legitimate, accredited, institution. Similarly, the federal government reserves its student-aid funds for students attending accredited schools. This chapter explores valuable resources for information on accreditation, plus several online indices to distance-education programs.

Council for Higher Education Accreditation
www.chea.org

The "directories" section of this site is the best resource for determining the legitimacy of an online degree program. It provides a list of accrediting agencies recognized by CHEA and the U.S. Department of Education. If a program is accredited by an unfamiliar agency, you can use these directories to determine whether that agency is, in fact, nationally recognized.

I can't stress enough how important it is to be sure your distance-education program is accredited by an agency recognized by the Department of Education or the Council for Higher Education Accreditation. Seedy Web sites keep cropping up, posing as accredited distance-learning programs. They'll tell you they are accredited, when in reality they have been 'accredited' by a less-than-respectable organization. Don't be fooled into throwing away thousands of dollars on a worthless degree.

Distance Education and Training Council
www.detc.org

This site is home to the DETC, an information clearinghouse for the distance education field. Founded in 1926, DETC also sponsors a nationally-recognized accrediting agency that evaluates specialized distance-education programs (those with no ties to traditional universities). Go to "Accredited Institutions" and browse the directory of available programs.

World Wide Learn
www.worldwidelearn.com

This gem of a website features a directory of hundreds of e-learning courses in 249 subject areas, as well as helpful articles about accreditation and how to choose the right online program. Started in 1998 and based in Canada, this site now boasts that it has the largest directory of online education in the world.

Peterson's Distance Learning
www.petersons.com/distancelearning

Conduct searches for full degree programs or single courses in this comprehensive database. You can even search by keyword. Try "nutrition," for example, and it returns nine schools, complete with in-depth descriptions, contact information and "facts and figures" (including course price tags).

Globewide Network Academy
www.gnacademy.org

As a resource for exploring the ins and outs of distance-education courses, from kindergarten through doctoral programs, the GNA is worth a look. It features a catalog of more than 32,000 distance-education courses offered throughout the world. The site, which is operated by a non-profit organization, emphasizes that it is a "listing service" only; it does not handle admissions or course registration. For that, you must contact schools directly. GNA also links you to other distance-ed lists and resources.

If you think you may eventually attend a "traditional" college, be sure to ask potential schools whether you can transfer your distance-education credits.

DANTES
www.dantes.doded.mil

The Defense Activity for Non-Traditional Education Support (DANTES) mission is to support off-duty (voluntary) education programs of the Department of Defense. The DANTES Distance Learning Program is primarily for military personnel whose schedules or duty locations do not permit traditional classroom attendance. The DANTES web site contains a great deal of information on distance learning, as well as a course catalogue of nationally-accredited distance learning degree programs.

Virtual University Gazette
www.geteducated.com/vugaz.htm

This monthly electronic newsletter is delivered free via e-mail to anyone who wishes to subscribe. Each issue includes a summary of new distance learning programs and links to online learning hot spots. A directory at the Web site features undergraduate and graduate programs that have chosen to advertise.

Degree.Net
www.degree.net

An appealing site, with news about distance ed and links to useful resources as well as warnings about unscrupulous schools. Degree.Net also includes a searchable data base of 100 "great distance-learning schools" based on the information in "College Degrees by Mail and Internet," a long-running book written by an irreverent distance-ed guru named John Bear.

An overwhelming number of traditional colleges and universities are getting into the e-learning business. In fact, some of the world's most prestigious schools (including Columbia, Stanford, the University of Chicago and the London School of Economics) offer courses online in conjunction with Fathom.com or UNext.com.

Better yet, if you already know which institution you'd like to attend "virtually," go to that institution's home page and search on words like "distance education" or "online courses" to see if it offers such programs.

Yahoo!

dir.yahoo.com/Education/Distance_Learning

If you're still stuck, Yahoo's listings may help in your search. A new section called Yahoo! Education also provides an overview of online learning. Go to degrees.education.yahoo.com.

Alt.education.distance

The main newsgroup for distance education, may be worth a glance.

A Sampling of Distance-Ed Programs

The field of distance education has already become so crowded that to list all the available programs would fill another book. But here is a sampling of some of the larger and better-known programs that have arrived on the scene, listed alphabetically:

Capella University

www.capellauniversity.edu

One of the oldest distance-learning schools in the country, Capella offers graduate and undergraduate degrees in information technology as well as graduate degrees from schools of Education, Business, Human Services and Psychology. Accredited by the North Central Association of Colleges and Schools, a legitimate group that accredits hundreds of other traditional colleges.

CIC Course Share
www.cic.uiuc.edu

The institutions in the Big 10 Conference (schools like Indiana University and Ohio State) have long worked together to coordinate their academic offerings, and maximize faculty expertise. Now, they have expanded their efforts to include distance-ed courses that can be taken by students at any school within the program.

Online Learning at Parkland College
online.parkland.edu

Illinois's Parkland College offers hundreds of online courses as well as "Classmate" online peer tutoring and a variety of other student support services. Click on "Online Degree Options" and you'll get information about completing an associate's degree entirely online.

Jones International University
www.jonesinternational.edu

Jones offers degrees on the undergraduate and graduate level, and holds a cyber-graduation ceremony each year. "The University of the Web," as Jones once called itself, was the first online university to earn full accreditation—from the North Central Association of Colleges and Schools—triggering concern among traditional educators who weren't convinced that online programs offer the same quality of experience as face-to-face programs. Meanwhile, the number of online courses continues to grow.

The New School Online University
www.dialnsa.edu

The New School has always looked for alternative ways to provide liberal-arts education, and the school's cybercampus, now called The New School Online University, provides yet another. In the last few years, the college has set up a program that allows undergraduate students to earn liberal-arts degrees over the Internet. The University offers dozens of non-degree online course options as well. The school is accredited by the Middle States Association of Colleges and Secondary Schools.

Servicemembers Opportunity Colleges
www.soc.aascu.org

A consortium of approximately 1800 colleges that provide educational opportunities for servicemembers and their families, and help them earn college degrees, either on-campus, or on-line.

Southern Regional Electronic Campus

www.electroniccampus.org

An online "campus" providing courses and degree programs from scores of colleges and universities across the South. Take a peek at the current offerings or search for specific courses and degree programs.

SUNY Learning Network

sln.suny.edu

The State University of New York includes more than 40 campuses—but even if you cannot find a way to physically get to one of them, you still have a shot using the university's Learning Network. Its Web site offers a lot of information to help you get started, as well as a list of 60 online degree programs and 4,000 online course offerings.

The University of Phoenix

www.phoenix.edu

With over 210,000 enrolled students and over 17,000 faculty members, this for-profit university is turning heads throughout the higher-education community. It aims to give working adults a chance to pursue a degree without quitting their jobs or disrupting their schedules. Students attend classes at one of 150 satellite campuses or take distance-education courses. Over 100,000 degree-seeking students study online. The university is fully accredited.

Western Governors University

www.wgu.edu

Western Governors University—which opened in 1998 with much fanfare but few students—is a collaborative effort among dozens of states. The goal is to create an institution to serve working adults by offering them alternative ways to get college-level credentials and learn new skills. Despite its lofty tag line, however ("Education Without Boundaries"), WGU is really just a handy networked catalog of online programs offered by colleges and corporations throughout the participating states.

Cooperative Education

Many universities offer cooperative education programs, which enable students to alternate between periods of studying on campus and working, for a salary, at a job related to their career interests. Co-op programs can be an invaluable way to learn skills and earn money for school at the same time. Search the Web sites of colleges that interest you, using words like "co-op" and "cooperative education." Also, Yahoo! and other search engines provide dozens of links to colleges' co-op programs.

National Commission for Cooperative Education
www.co-op.edu

A good starting point for information on cooperative education. Includes illustrations of how Co-op works, as well as an online guide about the benefits of Co-op called "Gaining the Co-op Edge.

Cooperative Education and Internship Association
www.ceiainc.org

Make this your first stop to get an overview of co-op education. You'll find general information, online resources, and links to other co-op sites including state and regional co-op agencies.

The Cooperative Education Network
www.ocasppcp.uc.edu/home

Go here for links to over 120 schools in the Cooperative Education Network as well as articles on the benefits of co-op. (Note: Nearly 900 schools offer some sort of co-op program.)

The Co-op Student Handbook
www.coop.neu.edu

Click on "Cooperative Education" to read Northeastern University's terrific online guide for students interested in exploring co-op.

Antioch Center for Cooperative Education
www.antioch-college.edu/co_op/html/survival.html

Antioch College, a small liberal-arts college in Yellow Springs, Ohio, has pulled together a Web site rich in co-op information, including information on programs at Antioch, which prides itself on its cooperative education requirement.

Studentjobs.gov
studentjobs.gov/d_coop.asp

The federal government also sponsors cooperative education, with Uncle himself serving as the students' employer. This site, developed by the Office of Personnel Management (OPM), has pulled together information on federal co-op, as well as listings of government fellowships, grants, internships, and scholarships The site even helps students create a winning profile and resume.

PART THREE

Ready to Apply?

CHAPTER 7

■■■■■■■■■■■■■■■■■■■

THOSE STRESSFUL
STANDARDIZED TESTS

Getting Organized

Two tests strike fear into the hearts of most college-bound juniors and seniors: The SAT (which once stood for Scholastic Aptitude Test, then Scholastic Assessment Test, but now is just called the SAT) and the ACT (which once stood for American College Testing). Advanced Placement exams are no fun either. But by tapping into a variety of online resources, you can at least prepare yourself for the worst. For general information and registration forms, check the following sites.

College Admissions Tests and Related Aid

icpac.indiana.edu/publications/infoseries/
is-11.xml

Get some objective information about testing before jumping into the sites created by companies that are seeking to profit from your anxiety. Provided by the Indiana Career and Postsecondary Advancement Center.

SAT Dates

www.collegeboard.com/student/testing/sat/
calenfees.html

The College Board provides a chart with SAT registration deadlines and testing dates for the upcoming year.

Online SAT Registration

www.collegeboard.com/testing

If you plan to pay for the SAT by credit card, and don't qualify for any special waivers, here's a hassle-free way to register.

Educational Testing Service Network

www.ets.org

The Educational Testing Service (ETS) develops the SAT (among other tests) which is then administered by the College Board, a client of ETS. Its site includes sections for students, parents and educators, press releases, practice test questions, and lots of cross links to the College Board. A few years ago, when ETS found a flaw in a test question, the service posted an announcement here about how the error affected test-takers.

ACT's Web site

www.actstudent.org

This is the electronic gateway to information about the ACT, a competitor to the SAT. It offers test strategies and sample questions, as well as links to electronic college search and application sites.

ACT Assessment Test Dates

www.actstudent.org/regist/currentdates.html

Test dates, through Year 2004, plus information on when to take the test if you live outside the 50 states.

Registering for the ACT

www.actstudent.org/regist

Find links for online registration, telephone registration for repeat test-takers, standby testing information, a list of upcoming test dates and deadlines, and the locations of test centers near you.

Getting Prepped

Reduce your stress level a notch or two by reviewing vocabulary or taking some practice tests.

The Wordsmyth S.A.T. Dictionary

www.lightlink.com/bobp/wedt/sat.htm

A downloadable list of 2000 words and definitions that often appear on SATs. Words with asterisks appear the most frequently, based on a ten-year analysis of SAT tests. Use this to create your own flash-card sessions. Check out the site's "words of the week" and word-game contests too.

TestU

www.testu.com

To get to TestU's pre-collegiate prep area, click on the photo at the left of the page. Once you click around, you'll see the cost is $59.95 for 50 hours of customized test prep. Not free, but certainly much cheaper than Kaplan or the Princeton Review.

Here's how the service works: First, TestU gives you a diagnostic exam to assess your core skills and generate a personalized study plan. Next, TestU runs you through a series of specific math and vocabulary tutorials designed to address your particular weaknesses. Third, you'll take some practice tests, including full-length SATs. And finally, you'll receive a last minute review of test-taking strategies.

TestU offers a free SAT mini-test if you want to get an idea of how you might do on the real thing; the sampler includes explanations of the correct answers.

Peterson's Test Prep

www.petersons.com/testprepchannel

Peterson's has also developed an affordable ($295) online SAT Prep course. As with TestU (described above), you start by taking a diagnostic exam, and then proceed through a course which has been tailored to meet your specific needs.

Kaplan's Test Prep

www.kaptest.com

Kaplan, one of the biggest names in the test-prep business, requires you to register for this site. But once you've done so, Kaplan provides you with a free practice SAT, a monthly e-newsletter, admission information, and test-taking tips. Naturally, you can also buy books and sign up for pricey courses. Kaplan charges $349 for its online SAT prep course, and $799 for its in-person, classroom course.

The Princeton Review

www.princetonreview.com/college/testPrep

If you're just browsing, check the free articles on raising test scores and the in-depth reports on past tests. If you're willing to stick around, register your e-mail address and other contact information and you'll be able to take some sample tests. And if you're already paying big bucks to take a Princeton Review course, plug in your password to get to more advanced online services. You can also take on online course for $399. By mid-fall 2004, the company plans to offer test-prep via cell phone by delivering new SAT questions throughout the day. There are no details yet on which cell phone plans will offer this service.

College Power Prep
www.powerprep.com

More free SAT or ACT help, via the Laboratory and Tip of the Day.

The Study Hall
www.studyhall.com

The Study Hall features a mystery novella packed with SAT vocabulary words. It's not great literature, and its certainly not what people mean when they tell you, "The best way to prepare for the SAT is to read the classics," but it's a reasonably painless way to absorb some new vocabulary.

The College Board's SAT Prep Center
apps.collegeboard.com/satprep/index.jsp

The College Board used to claim the test wasn't coachable. Now it lets you take a free mini-SAT to determine where you need the most help, and will (happily) sell you targeted Math and Verbal PrepPacks (sets of real questions for $16.95 each) and a comprehensive SAT review course ($29.95).

APEX Learning—Online Courses for Advanced Placement Exams
www.apexlearning.com

It used to be that only kids at huge, well-to-do high schools were offered an array of AP courses. Now students anywhere in the country can take them on line—if they have Internet access and can afford to pay the tuition of $475 per student per 18-week semester. APEX Learning Inc. is offering online courses taught by trained AP teachers. If you enroll, be prepared to spend about 10-15 hours a week completing multimedia tutorials, reading study guides, and participating in online discussions.

The catch is that students who sign up for these courses have to be dedicated and self-motivating. Many students choose to take the courses in the summer, when their schedules are not quite so packed. And here's another caveat: Teachers who participated in a similar program in California said that the least successful students were those who did not get support from their hometown high schools. Check with your school to see if they encourage students to take such courses. Some school districts will even pick up the tab.

APEX also offers AP Exam review for just $59 per subject. The review includes diagnostic assessments and unlimited access to the company's exam review site.

AP Help from The College Board
www.collegeboard.com/student/testing/ap/about.html

You can also get AP exam help from the College Board. This site includes an online newsletter, exam information, sample tests and extensive lists of online resources that you can use for further study.

The New, New SAT

Beginning in March, 2005 the College Board will begin administering a completely revised version of the SAT. Students will no longer have to suffer with ridiculous : relationship :: Analogy : Questions, or Column A < = > Column B Quantitative Comparisons. But they will have to answer multiple-choice grammar questions, write an original essay, and be comfortable with a slightly-higher level of mathematical concepts, for example absolute value and radical equations (as well as other Algebra II-level teachings).

The High School Class of '06 will be the first group required to take this New, New SAT.

The New SAT
www.collegeboard.com/student/testing/newsat/about.html

The College Board offers students a preview of The New SAT, as well as samples of the new questions and essay topics.

The "Big Three" of test prep also have New SAT news and New SAT tips: The Princeton Review (www.princetonreview), Kaplan (www.kaptest.com) and Peterson's (www.petersons.com).

CHAPTER 8

■■■■■■■■■■■■■■■■■■■■

THE APPLICATION FORM

The Almost-Paperless Application

Everyone complains about applying to college, usually for two good reasons: Using a typewriter to fill out the applications is a real pain, and college essays always invite major writer's block.

Well, that writer's block will probably stick around, but thankfully the days of typing applications are nearly over. The Internet now lets you complete your applications online. Instead of spending time messing with typewriter ribbon and aligning forms to type on the dotted line, you can use that time to think more carefully about what you want to include on the forms in the first place. And in some cases, you won't even have to type your name, address, and social-security number over and over again—the online programs remember the information and fill it in for you.

Paperless applications are becoming more and more prevalent, especially at large state or private universities. In fact, many colleges now encourage students to use the Internet, instead of sending in paper—it's less work for them. Soon, some colleges may only accept online applications.

And here's another bonus: The most advanced systems are now error-proof—the computer program won't accept an entry unless it's filled in correctly. Many colleges have also sprung for online systems that include request forms, Web-based applications, and the ability to check back, using the Internet, to see if you have been accepted.

Some Caveats

Several caveats remain, however. Here are a few:

- In many cases, you still have to send a check for the cost of the application through the U.S. mail. (Although an increasing number of colleges are inviting you to use your credit card.) You often have to send your personal essays by mail as well.

- Several colleges suggest that you print out the application and mail it, too—just in case.
- Some application systems allow you to download application forms electronically but do not yet accept applications that are sent on line. You must print and mail them.
- The ease of the Internet can cause carelessness. Don't hit the "submit" button until you are absolutely sure the application is in perfect shape. Get your parents or counselors to look over your forms before you zap them into the admissions office's inbox. And never send in an essay without having someone else proofread it first.

In any downloading operation, be prepared for a long download time. I wouldn't try this during Internet rush hour (which is usually early evenings and weekend afternoons), because you might end up with a half-hour wait. For more help with downloading, see Appendix 2.

Online Applications

With Web-based forms, applications can truly be completed on line—you don't need paper, printers, or diskettes. Simply register, enter the data, and hit the "send" button.

College admission offices have been scrambling over the past few years to bring you this option and they now advertise them prominently on their admission Web pages. *Go to those pages first.* You'll probably find scads of helpful information—like deadlines and application guidelines—that will make the online application process a lot easier.

To get to a college's admission pages, go to a school's Web site, and look for areas called "Admissions," "Apply," or "For Prospective Students." If you don't see those, try searching on the word "admission."

If you are visiting a college Web site that doesn't mention online applications, however, you still have some semi-paperless options. First, the college might offer *electronic* applications—application forms that you download to your computer. In most cases, you can fill them out using word-processing programs or they come with their own word-processing software. In rare cases, you must still print them out and then fill them in the old-fashioned way.

Second, a smattering of rival companies have created electronic applications that could be used to apply to the colleges of your choice. Here are some of the biggies:

Apply Online
www.princetonreview.com/college/apply

The Princeton Review provides over 700 online applications. And its sophisticated system has two big advantages: You can create an "Application Profile" which then automatically inserts your personal data (including extracurricular activities, test scores and other educational qualifications) into individual college applications; and you can use the "Application Inspector" to double check that you haven't skipped any questions before you submit your forms. The company says it will not disclose any of your information without your permission.

CollegeNET's ApplyWeb Online Applications
www.applyweb.com

Nearly 500 colleges have signed up to create their online applications through ApplyWeb. You must first open an account to gain access to the applications, and CollegeNET warns that your chosen "User Name" will become part of your ID when you transmit your applications to the colleges. The lesson? Don't get too cutesy with your name selection.

> Save. Save. Save. Completing your work on a computer is always a risky proposition. The electricity might flicker or your little brother could yank out the phone line. Either way, the stress of applying to college is bad enough without the threat of a digital catastrophe. Many online forms offer buttons that enable you to save your work as you go, or save your work and come back to it later. Use them.

XAP Applications
www.xap.com/apply

XAP lets you apply to over 700 different colleges. As you finish each screen of an application, XAP checks your data for errors, omissions and inconsistencies, and saves your work as you go.

Next Stop College

www.collegeboard.com/apply

The College Board's online application service lets you personalize a "Desktop" to help you organize and prepare your college applications. It comes complete with checklists to keep you on track. Also, a small bonus, if you have taken the SAT already, the software will retrieve rote information—like your mailing address—from the College Board database and plop it into the form for you.

Colleges that cannot yet accept electronic applications may at least offer an electronic way to request the application forms, so that you can receive them via the U.S. Post Office. Look on Web sites like PrincetonReview.com or CollegeNET for links like "information request forms" or "request an application."

The Common Application

app.commonapp.org

The Common Application was developed so students would not have to fill out different applications for every school on their list. Instead, they complete this application once and send copies to participating colleges (although some schools require extra information, like an additional essay, supplemental activities sheets or answers to a few extra questions). If you are applying to one of these 255 colleges, you will find an online version of the application at this site, as well as links to these supplemental forms.

If you are applying to a selective college, and it has its own application (electronic- or paper-based), use it, even if the school says it accepts a generic form like the Common Application. Not only do these selective college applications often ask questions not found on more generic forms, but your willingness to complete a unique application indicates greater interest in the college. And with competitive admissions, you want to gain every advantage possible.

CHAPTER 9

■■■■■■■■■■■■■■■■■■■■■

ESSAYS, INTERVIEWS AND RECOMMENDATIONS

Ugh! The Essay

There is no easy way out of writing that personal essay, but some Internet tools can make your task a little less painful. Just be careful how you use them. Colleges are becoming increasingly wary over the proliferation of essay-writing "help" and online "cheating." Duke applications, for example, now make the following request: "We recognize that all good writers seek feedback, advice, or editing before sending off an essay. When your essay is complete, please answer the following: 'Whose advice did you seek for help with your answer? Was s/he helpful? What help did s/he provide?' "

Writing the College Admission Essay

icpac.indiana.edu/publications/infoseries/ is-15.xml

Some useful nuggets on choosing essay topics, being creative, composing your thoughts, and revising them, from the Indiana Career and Postsecondary Advancement Center. The ICPAC infoseries contains dozens of other equally-useful college planning articles.

IvyEssays

www.ivyessays.com

This company's slogan is "Inspiration by example," but many admission officers remain skeptical. The service is designed to provide—for a fee—copies of admission essays written by students who got into Ivy League colleges. But IvyEssays offers quite a bit of useful free advice, as well, to help you brainstorm your way to strong essay topics, create a variety of structured outlines, develop catchy lead in sentences, and hold your reader's attention until the end. Just for laughs, and reassurance, you should also read the section about funny mistakes that people have let slip into their masterpieces.

Site creators say they are simply showing students what it takes to write their own successful essays and emphasize the evils (and illegality) of plagiarism. Admissions officers and others say, "au contraire," and think this can be a gateway to plagiarism. Plus, they are starting to get savvy. If you simply re-use an essay from this site, chances are the admission officers have seen it already and they'll reject you outright. If you want to shell out cash for this service, use it honestly.

EssayEdge

www.essayedge.com

Online tips and quizzes to help you think about your accomplishments, select strong essay topics, and write excellent essays. The free "Essay Help Course" contains six lessons to take you through the whole process: (1) Preparation; (2) Question-Specific Strategies; (3) Structure and Outline; (4) Style and Tone; (5) Introductions and Conclusiosns; and (6) Editing and Revising. Of course, like other essay-service sites, the editors at EssayEdge would be happy to help you polish your final product ... for a fee.

Cambridge Essay Service

www.world.std.com/~edit

This site is mostly geared to those poor saps willing to spend $250 - $600 to get help writing their essays. I'd suggest skipping anything with a price tag and heading for the free stuff—"Seven Great Tips" on writing a good essay.

Useful References For Any Writer

The Wordsmyth Educational Dictionary-Thesaurus

www.wordsmyth.net

Unsure of a word's spelling? Confused about a word's meaning? This new online dictionary is a quick way to find answers. Plus, it offers synonyms for all its entries.

Thesaurus.com and Dictionary.com

www.thesaurus.com and www.dictionary.com

You can't beat these sites for their easy-to-remember Web addresses and easy-to-use features. For example, the online version of Roget's Thesaurus lets you type a word similar to the one evading you, and see what pops up. They are both great resources for daily crosswords and word puzzles too.

The Slot

www.theslot.com

Tongue-in-cheek grammar tips from Bill Walsh, a very witty (and opinionated) copy editor at *The Washington Post,* and author of *The Elephants of Style.* The Slot covers word choice, punctuation, quotations, capitalization, spelling, style and more.

The Elements of Style

www.bartleby.com

This site provides an online version of the first edition of this writing classic, by William Strunk, Jr. (To find it, select "Strunk's Style" under the list of references.) It's a must read before starting any big writing assignment like your college essays. Learn how to use the active voice, omit needless words, avoid commonly misspelled words, and more.

Bartleby's also includes the full texts of nearly a hundred other classic references, including *Robert's Rules of Order, Emily Post on Etiquette, Gray's Anatomy, The* (King James) *Bible, Bartlett's Quotations, Bullfinch's Mythology, The Columbia Encyclopedia*, and the 18-volume *Cambridge History of English and American Literature.*

Don't Forget the Interview...

Even in this electronic era, the face-to-face interview holds weight at some schools. The admissions pages of most colleges will tell you whether an interview is required or suggested. If an admissions office offers an e-mail address on its Web page, feel free to send a note asking about scheduling one. Then, make it the last stop on your campus tour.

The Princeton Review's interview Advice

www.princetonreview.com/college

Here you will find a series of feature articles on the admissions process, including the interview. Click there and tap into some smart advice, including essays on what to wear, and what NOT to talk about.

Your Virtual Interview

www.bergen.org/AAST/Projects/CollegePrep/interview.html

This site offers some useful suggestions, then allows you to practice your conversation skills with a ten-question virtual interview.

College Admission Office E-Mail Addresses

www.college-scholarships.com

Scroll down to "Colleges by State." Schools are listed alphabetically (by state) with clickable icons for their admission (and financial-aid) offices.

> If you are not working at your own computer, be careful about sending e-mail messages directly from the Web. Here's why: Web browsers are usually set to a specific e-mail address—in this case, not your own. Let's say you send a message from a computer at cyberbar@state.com. The recipient is likely to "reply to sender." That reply will go straight to cyberbar@state.com, and you may never know whether you received a response. A good rule of thumb, whether writing e-mails from home or elsewhere, is to sign messages with your e-mail address as well as your name. That way, message recipients will know how to get in touch.

Dealing with Recommendations

Few online applications are sophisticated enough to handle online recommendations. Your best bet is to follow the directions on the application itself—whether it is electronic or in print. You may want to ask, however, whether the admission office will take recommendations via e-mail. If the person writing the letter is comfortable with e-mail—and the office receiving the letter is also comfortable with the idea—then it may be easier for everyone involved.

The Secondary School Report Form

www.nacac.com/downloads.html

This form, at least, is available online. It's for high-school guidance counselors only and must carry the high school's official seal once it is printed and filled out. The form is usually attached to the student's admission application before it is sent.

National Association for College Admission Counseling

www.nacac.com

High-school counselors might want to take a peek at NACAC's main site. It is designed for college admissions officers, but also provides information and forms for those in the secondary-school arena.

PART FOUR

∎∎∎∎∎∎∎∎∎∎∎∎∎∎∎∎∎∎∎∎∎∎

Financial Aid—The Wired Way

CHAPTER 10

■■■■■■■■■■■■■■■■■■■■■■■■

FINANCIAL-AID OVERVIEW

You've heard the horror stories. Tuition costs are rising at twice the rate of inflation, and students and parents are buckling down for decades of debt. But don't let the hype keep you from finding a way to make college affordable. Beyond the extremes of $35,000 price tags and impossible loan burdens (neither of which are as common as you think) you will find plenty of reasonably priced colleges, low-interest loans, and some shots at scholarships.

Several Internet sites make the financial-aid process much easier. You'll find everything from federal student-aid applications to advice on saving tuition money.

Thinking Ahead

Get in financial-planning mode, but don't worry about digging around for a calculator. Many Web sites now provide online calculators and other interactive devices that crunch the numbers for you.

Kiplinger's Personal Finance Magazine
www.kiplinger.com

This site, produced by the personal-finance magazine, offers several worthwhile areas. First, go to the calculators section (under "Tools"), scroll down to "Planning Tools" and look for "How do I Figure a Monthly College Savings Plan?" and "What will it take to save for a college education?" You'll get a sophisticated tool that tells you (1) how much you'll need to sock away each month to reach your college savings goal, and (2) what you'll need to change about your current plan to keep pace with rising college prices (e.g., increase your monthly investment by $75).

You'll also find *Kiplinger's* rankings of the best values in public and private colleges and "Section 529" college savings plans, as well as numerous other tidbits that have appeared in the print version of the magazine over the past few years.

Money 101 — Saving for College

money.cnn.com/pf/101/lessons/11

Test your financial savvy when it comes to saving for your children's college education. *Money Magazine's* "Saving for College" lesson includes numerous background articles and a quiz that will put you in the mindset. For more information, type "colleges" into the site's search box and retrieve articles, online calculators, and databases.

Smart Money Magazine

www.smartmoney.com/college

The College Planning section of *Smart Money's* personal finance site includes long- and short-term savings strategies, recommended portfolios (based on the student's expected enrollment date), "529 Plan" calculators and much more.

Financial Aid Calculators

www.finaid.org/calculators

Mark Kantrowitz, developer of the enormously useful FinAid page described in the next section, has designed over 25 free calculators for you to use on line (as well as links to dozens more). For example, *College Cost Projector* estimates how much college will cost in the future. *Savings Growth Projector* shows how your current investment fund will do. *Savings Plan Designer* suggests how much you should save each month to pay your college bills.

Student Loan Advisor helps you determine how much you'll be able to repay each month (based on the kind of job you're seeking). *Loan Comparison Calculator* lets you see which loan is "the best deal."

And the *Financial Aid Estimation Form* previews how much Uncle Sam will expect your family to contribute to college costs.

Parents: Don't let results from overly simplistic "How Much You Need to Save" calculators scare you off. They were popularized by greedy investment companies which are all-too-happy to take your money and manage it for you. Remember, you don't pay 100% of a four-year college bill the day your student enrolls. The bills are spread out over four years, so make sure your calculator reflects this longer time-line. Also, you can supplement your savings with a contribution from income and a small loan. A more realistic goal would be to save enough to cover half your expected college costs.

The College Board's Financial Aid Services
www.collegeboard.com/pay

A good overview of savings options as well as a realistic look at what colleges actually cost (most people overestimate the expense) and calculators to help you determine your parents' capacity to take on additional debt, how much your college savings will grow over time, and more.

Investment Advice
Fidelity (www.fidelity.com)
Morningstar (www.morningstar.com)
Vanguard (www.vanguard.com)
The Street (www.thestreet.com)
Quicken (www.quicken.com)
The Motley Fool (www.fool.com)

Most mutual fund companies, as well as the major investment sites, also provide planning tools for people trying to pay for college. If you have several years before tuition bills are due, you might take a peek at the college planning sections of the sites above.

Financial Aid 101

There is more than $100 billion available in student aid and education tax credits, most of which comes from Uncle Sam. The rest comes from your home state, your college, your employer, your parents' employer, and a small percent from private scholarships. And how do you get all this aid? Apply. Apply. Apply.

As you wander through the net you will see several offers for free money, scholarships, and—yes—scams. So before you get caught up in that stuff, head for . . .

FinAid! The Smart Student's Guide to Financial Aid
www.finaid.org

This site is brimming with valuable stuff—updates on just-released reports, answers to frequently asked questions, calculators for determining costs, and links to most aid resources (federal, state, collegiate, and private). Published by Mark Kantrowitz, a computer scientist and author with a wealth of knowledge on the subject, it looks at financial aid from the students' and parents' points of view.

Students.Gov

www.students.gov

This site was designed to be a 24/7 "student gateway to the US government." Its collection of sites helps students find a job (or internship), e-file taxes, plan vacations, register to vote, buy postage stamps, and plan and pay for a college education. Link to electronic applications, loan information, and financial aid opportunities organized by state.

College Is Possible

www.collegeispossible.org

This site is part of the response to a major study showing how mis-informed most people are about college costs and the availability of financial aid. The resource section is divided into three main parts: (1) Preparing for College; (2) Choosing the Right College; and (3) Paying for College. The site is sponsored by dozens of associations connected to post-secondary education, and is intended to disabuse families of all their misconceptions about college.

Many computers come with Adobe Acrobat Reader pre-installed, but if yours doesn't, you can download the software for free. Go to www.adobe.com for more information, or find help in Appendix 2.

FastWeb's Parents Page

www.fastweb.monster.com/fastweb/content/parents/index.ptml

Get answers about college financing from FastWeb, a well-respected—and huge—scholarship data base. Ask questions of financial experts and read about scholarship strategies.

Wired Scholar, From Sallie Mae

www.wiredscholar.com

This financial aid site touches on myriad topics, and is brought to you by Sallie Mae, the huge student-loan company. Read about how the loan process works, how to pick a lender and how to borrow responsibly.

Mapping Your Future

www.mapping-your-future.org/paying

Sponsored by a group of more than 30 state loan agencies who guarantee Federal Family Education Loans against default, this site provides all sorts of college and career advice (in English and in Spanish) to parents, students, and those who already have loans.

To get in touch with the loan agency in your state, go to mapping-your-future.org/about/sponsors.cfm, where you'll find links to their Web pages, organized alphabetically. Here are a few that are especially rich in information:

California Student Aid Commission

www.csac.ca.gov
www.edfund.org

Illinois Student Assistance Commission

www.collegezone.org

Texas Guarantee Student Loan Corporation

www.tgslc.org
www.AdventuresinEducation.org

Soc.college.financial-aid

Most newsgroup messages, including ones posted to this group, are of widely varying quality. Some are simply advertisements for investment services or fee-based scholarship searches on which you shouldn't waste much time or money. Some, however, contain specific questions that might be on your mind as well. Once in a while, experts reply to these questions out of the goodness of their hearts—and the answers can be useful. If you don't see an answer to your own question, feel free to post it. (For more information on newsgroups, see Appendix 2.)

Applying for Financial Aid

The only way to get federal-, state- or collegiate-based financial aid is to apply for it. In all instances, you'll need to complete a Free Application for Federal Student Aid (FAFSA). If you've set your sights on an expensive private school, you'll probably have to complete the College Board's PROFILE, as well. In completing these applications, you enable the school's financial aid administrator to learn how much your family can contribute to college costs, and how much you will need in financial aid.

Expected Family Contribution

www.collegeboard.com/pay

Under "Calculators," the College Board allows you to estimate your "Expected Family Contribution" using the Federal Methodology and the Institutional Methodology to learn (in advance) what the federal government and others think you can reasonably pay, out of your own pocket, toward college costs each year. The Federal Methodology is actually set by Uncle Sam, so assuming you plug in the same family income and asset data, your result SHOULD be the same, regardless of whether you use the College Board's version, or one sponsored by a lending institution (see below). The Institutional Methodology is a more comprehensive formula developed by The College Board (with input from the colleges) to determine your eligibility for non-federal aid, for example, collegiate scholarships.

> The Federal Methodology is applied to income and asset data you submit on the FAFSA. (More information on federal financial aid is available in the next chapter.) The Institutional Methodology is applied to income and asset data you submit on the PROFILE (or a college's own aid application).

FAFSA on the Web

www.fafsa.ed.gov

Paper FAFSAs still work fine, but an electronic version is available as well. To complete the application online, make sure your Web browser is Netscape Navigator 6.2 or above, or Microsoft Internet Explorer 5.0 or above.

When you're finished, you can either print and mail a separate signature page or use your "Personal Identification Number" (PIN) to verify your identity (and, later, check on the status of your aid application).

> If possible, request a PIN from the Department of Education (www.pin.ed.gov) and complete your FAFSA on line. Not only will your application get processed faster, but internal edits will cut down on mistakes. If your parents are required to sign the FAFSA, they will need their own (separate) PIN.

Also, make sure to save a personal copy of your FAFSA—a step often forgotten by people who fill forms out on line. But don't use the save function listed under your Web browser's pull-down menu—you'll be saving an unprotected (i.e., unencrypted) copy that someone could use to view your personal information. Instead, use the save buttons at the bottom of each screen.

Don't be confused by www.FAFSA.com. This enterprising financial aid consultant nabbed a prime domain name, but charges families $79.99 to complete the forms. You can do it yourself for free. Your choice.

PROFILE
profileonline.collegeboard.com

Many schools and scholarship programs require additional information about your family's finances to help them award non-federal aid. They sign contracts with the College Scholarship Service (the financial-aid division of the College Board) to gather this data via PROFILE. Through this site you can register for PROFILE and fill the forms out online. To complete these Web-based forms, however, you must be running an advanced Web browser.

Ask your parents to start work on their 2004 taxes as soon as possible. Not only will it be much easier to complete the FAFSA and PROFILE, but their income data on all these forms must match pretty closely.
The 2005-2006 PROFILE will be available on October 1, 2004; the 2005-2006 FAFSA will not be available until January 1, 2005.

CHAPTER 11

■■■■■■■■■■■■■■■■■■■■■■■

FEDERAL STUDENT AID

Pell Grants, Supplemental Educational Opportunity Grants, Work-Study, Stafford Loans, PLUS Loans, Perkins Loans. Through these six gigantic programs, Uncle Sam funds over $60 billion in student aid every year.

The Student Guide
www.studentaid.ed.gov/guide

This site is a must. *The Student Guide* walks you through the application process, telling you more than you ever wanted to know about the FAFSA, which stands for Free Application for Federal Student Aid, and the six federal grant and loan programs mentioned above. **You can view this guide in either English or Spanish.**

Office of Postsecondary Education (OPE)
www.ed.gov/about/offices/list/OPE/index.html

If you want to learn the nitty-gritty details behind student-aid initiatives, stop here for financial-aid news, program highlights, reference materials, and links to OPE's partners in education and government.

More on Loans

Federal student loans are dispensed under two parallel systems: 1) the Federal Direct Student Loan Program (Direct Lending), in which your loan is made by the federal government directly; and 2) Federal Family Education Loan Program (FFEL) in which your loans come from commercial lenders, such as banks and credit unions. In either case, eligibility, loan limits and interest rates are equivalent, and determined by the federal government. If you apply for federal aid, your college will probably tell you which route to take (some schools participate in direct lending; others do not). In some cases, however, you may be faced with a decision. Which system is better?

This is not an idle question. Legislators, lobbyists, and Department of Education officials have been debating this for the past decade. Private lenders, which make money off the interest subsidies (and gain potential young customers for other banking services), are no fans of direct lending. It cuts them out of the picture. They also say customer service will suffer if the government takes over and the competition among lenders is eliminated. The Clinton Administration, on the other hand, favored the program, claiming it was more efficient and a better use of taxpayer money.

The Bush Administration hasn't fiddled much with the program, so for now, direct lending and commercial lenders co-exist—with students getting the best end of the deal: better service and better repayment terms, bred by the competition among everybody to prove which system is more efficient. The following sites are most valuable for their information on loans, application deadlines, and repayment plans. But, in the midst of it all, they also offer partisan accounts of both sides of the direct-lending debate.

The Direct Loan Program

www.ed.gov/DirectLoan

Head for the section titled "About Direct Loans," which describes the different types of direct loans, outlines your repayment options, and tells you what will happen if you don't pay off your loan. Under "External Sites," you can link to the home pages of Direct Loan schools. This site is sponsored by the U.S. Department of Education.

eStudent Loan

www.estudentloan.com

There is nothing better than being able to compare a half dozen loan programs side-by-side to see which ones offer the best deals. Visit LoanFinder on this site to do just that. To get started, you must sign up for a username and password, but after that, the process is quite straightforward. First, you answer a few basic questions, and decide which features are most important to you (for example, lowest APR or lowest overall payment). Then, LoanFinder displays the "best" matches, including links to lender Web sites so you can apply online.

One drawback: LoanFinder only displays a few of the available options (generally less than four), so you can't be certain which loans have been evaluated. Furthermore, some of the biggest lenders do not participate in the service, so if you rely exclusively on LoanFinder you may miss the best deal. This is especially true for students who live in a state that sponsors low-interest loans.

Sallie Mae

www.salliemae.com

Sallie Mae has provided funds for education loans (primarily federal student loans) for over thirty years, and now either owns or manages over $72 billion in loans for more than seven million borrowers. The Sallie Mae Web site answers questions about the corporation itself and provides checklists on what to look for in lenders. Not surprisingly, Sallie Mae wants students to use lenders that have partnerships with itself. It offers a "lender locator," as well as online calculators to help you shop for the best repayment plan, and figure out the cost of your loan.

 Sallie Mae purchased USA Group in July, 2000 and the two organizations have integrated most of their education loans operations as well as their web sites.

Banks, Guaranty Agencies, and More

Yahoo!'s List of Lenders

dir.yahoo.com/Education/Financial_Aid/Loans

An ever-expanding list of lenders, compiled by Yahoo!. You'll find links to banks and other lenders that offer online information about student aid and their educational funding programs. Many of these lenders provide federally-guaranteed loans and give you online access to your loan account. Eventually, you will be able to apply using the FAFSA. For now, you have to contact the lender, and complete a very simple separate application. Most big lenders have now put their loan applications on line.

What follows (in alphabetical order) is a partial list of banks and agencies that provide educational funding, and a wealth of useful college-related information—more financial-aid tips, more information on loan consolidation, more links to student-aid sites, and more calculators to help you determine your best repayment option.

If there is a particular bank you trust for checking or credit-card accounts, you may want to take a look at their student-aid offerings too.

Access Group

www.accessgroup.org

ASAP/Union Bank & Trust

www.asapubt.com

Bank of America
www.bankofamerica.com/studentbanking

Bank One
www.educationone.com

Chase Bank
www.chase.com/educationfirst

Chela Financial Services
www.loans4students.org

Citibank
www.studentloan.com

Educaid (Owned by Wachovia)
www.educaid.com

Fleet
www.fleet.com/education

Key Education Resources
www.key.com/education

LoanStar Education Loans
www.loanstar.com

National City
www.nationalcity.com

PNC Bank
www.eduloans.pncbank.com

Southwest Student Services Corporation
www.sssc.com

Student Loan Funding
www.studentloanfunding.org

SunTrust Bank
www.suntrusteducation.com

US Bank
www.usbank.com/studentloans

Wells Fargo
wellsfargo.com/per/accounts/student

Loan Locator
www.nslc.org

Most banks sell their loans, which means you may get your loan from one institution, but repay it to another. Of course, you are supposed to be notified of this switcheroo, however, if you lose track of your lender, try this nifty service under the "student" section of The National Student Loan Clearinghouse.

State Guaranty Agencies
bcol02.ed.gov/Programs/EROD/org_list.cfm

Look down the list of organizations in this Education Resource Directory and click on "State Guaranty Agencies." If by some chance you cannot find a lender, contact your state agency. It will either make the loan or point you in the right direction.

As you shop around for your student loan, look carefully at repayment options—you'll find real differences. For example, some lenders will refund your 3% origination fee. Others reward you for making on-time payments. Common bonuses: forgiving your last six payments or knocking 2% off your interest rate.

Tax Cuts Explained
(Or, How Do I Get HOPE?)

In August, 1997, Congress passed a tax-relief act that was chock full of educational tax credits and deductions, plus more flexible rules concerning Individual Retirement Accounts (IRAs). The most publicized part of this bill was the HOPE Scholarship program, in which certain taxpayers receive a $1,500 tuition credit for the first two years of post-secondary school. Many parents are now seeing the benefits—if they can figure it all out.

Since then, Congress has approved several additional rounds of tax cuts which expand existing incentives and introduce a few new treats, like a deduction for education expenses. The following Web pages should help you keep it all straight.

The HOPE Scholarship and Lifetime Learning Credits
www.ed.gov/offices/OPE/PPI/HOPE

Visit the U.S. Department of Education's guide to the HOPE scholarship, lifetime learning credits, education savings accounts, and more. Take a look at the *Families' Guide to the 1997 Tax Cuts for Education.* Or, if you'd like to torture yourself with government jargon, head for the full texts of the law as well as IRS notices and regulations.

Economic Growth and Tax Relief Reconciliation Act of 2001

www.house.gov/rules/1836_sum.pdf

The Economic Growth and Tax Relief Reconciliation Act of 2001 introduced a new tax deduction for qualified higher education expenses and expanded benefits for state-based college savings plans (see Chapter 12) and Coverdell Education Savings Plans (formerly Education IRAs). It also raised qualifying income limits for several existing tax-relief programs and expanded the income exclusion for employer-paid tuition to include graduate studies. If you can't wait for all the analysis, you can go straight to the bill itself, or read this fifteen-page summary.

The Motley Fool

www.fool.com/taxes/taxcenter

The Motley Fool's TaxCenter includes many articles which will help you understand the impact of the Taxpayer Relief Act of 1997, the Tax Relief Extension Act of 1999, the Economic Growth and Tax Relief Reconciliation Act of 2001, and the Jobs and Growth Tax Reconciliation Act of 2003.

Tax Benefits for Education

www.irs.gov/individuals/students/index.html

www.irs.gov/pub/irs-pdf/p970.pdf

Tax information straight from the horse's mouth. In reviewing these sites, remember they are valuable for their factual information, not their consumer insights.

CHAPTER 12

■ ■

BEYOND UNCLE SAM

After you've figured out how federal loan programs work, take a look at what your state offers, what your prospective college might make available, and what private loan programs are out there.

State Aid

Among states, the numbers and types of scholarship and loan programs vary widely—and new programs such as prepaid tuition plans are popping up everywhere. In most cases, you must be an in-state resident planning to attend an in-state public college to be eligible for this assistance.

State Education Agencies and Higher-Education Agencies
bcol02.ed.gov/Programs/EROD/org_list.cfm

Scroll through the directory and look for these two resource lists. "State Education Agencies" links you to each state's main education office; "State Higher Education Agencies" takes you to each state's higher education commission. Go to the main education department pages for information about the state's policies on everything from K-12 to higher education. Go to the higher education commission for information on specific loan and scholarship packages, as well as other assistance programs for college-bound students.

College Savings Plans Network
www.collegesavings.org

To encourage early planning for college, every state now sponsors at least one type of college savings programs:

(1) Prepaid Tuition Plans allow parents to guarantee four years of tuition at any of the state's public (or in some cases private) schools by making a lump sum investment of periodic payments.

(2) Savings Plan Trusts give families tax incentives to save for college.

No two programs are the same, and many are not restricted to state residents, so shop around. This site, sponsored by the National Association of State Treasurers, will link you to individual state plans and update you on all the newly-enacted tax incentives (in short, earnings from these plans are now exempt from federal income tax).

The Internet Guide to 529 Plans
www.savingforcollege.com

Qualified tuition programs (which consist primarily of state-based college savings plans and prepaid tuition plans) are also known as "529 Plans," named for the section of the tax code which clarifies their tax-favored status. Compiled by two CPAs from New York, this site offers state-by-state comparisons and ratings to help you figure out which plan is best for your family's situation. Plans are evaluated based on their flexibility, liquidity, financial aid impact, investment approach, and extra (state) benefits. This last item is especially important—most plans are open to residents of every state, however, they reserve their best terms for locals.

Collegiate Aid

Be sure to visit the financial-aid Web pages of colleges you are considering. These provide three essentials in your financial-aid quest:

- Information on scholarship and loan programs specific to that college
- Notices of critical deadlines
- News on tuition rates and payment plans.

Here are some easy ways to find them:

Financial Aid Office Web Pages
www.finaid.org/otheraid/fao.phtml

The FinAid site comes through again. You'll find a fairly comprehensive directory of financial-aid offices—including web sites, e-mail addresses, postal addresses, and phone numbers.

College and University Aid Offices
www.yahoo.com/Education/Financial_Aid

Yahoo!'s list. Easy to find, but not terribly comprehensive.

If you do not see the college you want listed on the pages above, go to the college's home page. If the home page does not mention financial aid, try sections labeled "admissions," "for entering students" or "student information."

Focusing on Scholarships

You will find links to these sites on most pages that describe financial aid. The sites have earned reputations for being helpful and free. And because they are helpful and free, there is little reason for you to pay money for some other scholarship search—so don't get suckered by Web sites that ask you to do just that.

FastWeb
www.fastWeb.monster.com

Financial Aid Search Through the Web. Set aside some time to go through this site, which provides information on nearly 600,000 scholarship opportunities. You have to register, but the site's producers are honest about telling you that some of the information you supply is given to colleges and "marketing partners." Then fill out the registration pages, being careful not to sign up for any music clubs or magazine subscriptions. . . unless you want to.

You will then wait for a few minutes, while the site pulls its customized information together. The results are worth the wait. You'll find information on scholarships, fellowships, internships, and loans. You can go back to the site every few weeks to see if there are any new opportunities that fit your profile. You will also receive e-mail messages alerting you to new scholarships that match your search criteria. And you get a bonus—each of the entries gives you an overview of the award and several options, depending on the award: (1) Go to the sponsor's Web site for more information; (2) Send an e-mail to the sponsor requesting additional information; (3) Create a customized letter (to snail mail to the sponsor) requesting more information and a paper application; or (4) Apply online.

MACH25
www.collegenet.com/mach25

Like FastWeb, this site boasts of 600,000 scholarships, however, you don't need to fill out a lengthy questionnaire or divulge any personal information to access them. Instead, you can browse through all the awards, or view them by keyword, for example, "yearbook" or "journalism" or "sports"and decide for yourself which ones are relevant.

Scholarship Search

www.collegeboard.com/pay

This free Web version of the College Board's FUND FINDER scholarship database contains annually-updated information on scholarships and fellowships from more than 2,300 sources. You don't need to register any personal contact information; just answer questions about your affiliations and interests, and your results appear almost immediately. In a test search, the matches were highly relevant to the entered criteria.

High-school guidance counselors can get more information about ExPAN's extensive database system from www.collegeboard.com/expan/html/features.html. ExPAN maintains information on scholarships, electronic applications, career information, and more.

> Sometimes when you click on a link, an entirely new browser window will open up on your computer screen. Many new sites include this feature, which lets you to click around on one page, without losing track of the index page on which you started. You may find yourself with several open windows, however. Close them when you have finished browsing to keep yourself organized.

WiredScholar (from Sallie Mae)

www.wiredscholar.com

You'll find a scholarship search in the right-hand column. It takes just a few minutes to complete a profile form, and once you click the submit button, you can view your results almost immediately, or you can pay ScholarshipExperts.com $29.95 for a more intensive search (and tools that make it easier to apply for awards).

Sallie Mae promises that it will not sell or rent your contact information to third-party vendors, like unwanted advertisers.

Pacific Northwest Scholarship Guide

www.collegeplan.org/cpnow/pnwguide/pnwguide.htm

If you live in the Pacific Northwest, don't miss this site. The searchable scholarship guide gives you information on hundreds of scholarships available to students who go to school in the Northwest or have parents who work at companies based there.

The Scholarship Research Network

www.srnexpress.com

This Maryland-based company offers a free (express) service which is worth trying. You'll have to register, and give out your phone number, but if you do, you'll get to search a fairly comprehensive scholarship database including facts about eligibility, deadlines, and application information.

The United Negro College Fund

www.uncf.org

The UNCF offers a clearinghouse of hundreds of scholarships that can be redeemed at its member colleges, most of which are located in the Southeast (from Virginia to Texas) and were historically-black institutions. You can download the scholarship application straight from the site, but to qualify you must have at least a 2.5 GPA.

The UNCF also administers the $1 billion Gates Millennium Scholarship Program (www.gmsp.org) for low-income minority students and provides details on more than 1000 other scholarships that primarily serve African-American students.

Black Excel

www.blackexcel.org

Click on the scholarship gateway for information about the above programs, plus more than a dozen other links to scholarships for Native American and African-American students.

American Society of Association Executives

www.asaenet.org

Many organizations provide scholarships to future members. Under "Directories" go to "Associations" for a gateway and Web-links to over 10,000 associations. Search for career fields that interest you, click to that association's home page, and learn more about its annual conference, student chapters, and scholarship programs.

The Foundation Center
www.fdncenter.org/funders

You won't find a scholarship search, just links to more than 70,000 private foundations and 2,400 corporate grant-makers that may award funds for projects in your area of interest.

Don't Get Scammed

The Internet is riddled with offers that are a complete waste of money. Fortunately, it also provides sites that warn you about them.

Scholarship Scams
www.ftc.gov/bcp/conline/edcams/scholarship

Set up by the Federal Trade Commission, this page offers some tips on spotting scholarship scams.

Evaluating Scholarship Matching Services
www.finaid.org/scholarships/matching.phtml

Another valuable service from FinAid. Helps you evaluate scholarship services and provides advice on protecting yourself from scams.

> Don't mistake a strange suffix like .phtml or .shtml—or even .asp?—for a typo. As the Web becomes more advanced, so does the code behind it. These suffixes are signals telling the Web site to load pages a particular way.

Considering the Military...

The U.S. Military will generously help you pay for college—if you agree to serve in some capacity for a few or more years. All branches offer ROTC scholarships and let you build (sizable) college funds via the Montgomery GI Bill. Currently, you may receive over $35,000 in education benefits for a three- or four-year enlistment.

The Army sweetens the pot further with its Army College Fund if you enlist in certain "Military Occupation Specialties." (The Navy and Marine Corps have similar benefits.) The Army will also repay up to $65,000 of your federal student loans.

Military.Com

www.military.com/Careers/Education

An extensive career and education resource center from "Military Advantage," a privately-funded company targeting the military community. You'll get information on the GI Bill, ROTC, and scholarships for Veterans.

ROTC Headquarters

www.defenselink.mil/faq/pis/19.html

Addresses, phone numbers and Web links.

The GI Bill

www.gibill.va.gov

Everything there is to know about the GI Bill, courtesy of Uncle Sam.

My Future

www.myfuture.com

The U.S. Armed Forces have collaborated on a Web site. Here, you'll get an overview of educational (and career) benefits and links to each service.

...or Community Service

Volunteering now brings more than just emotional fulfillment. Do good work and you can earn money for college or forgiveness for some of your student loans.

AmeriCorps, and the Corporation for National Service

www.americorps.org

www.nationalservice.org

AmeriCorps participants receive a modest living allowance, health insurance, and a $4,725 credit per year of full-time service (for a maximum of two years). They may use the credit at any college or graduate school, or to pay off their outstanding student loans. Each year, 50,000 students serve in over 2,000 locally-run programs across the United States and their work includes mentoring, disaster relief, and helping to close the digital divide. At the corporation's site, you can look through the AmeriCorps Program Directory to find a project that interests you. You can also link to dozens of other worthy organizations that could use your time (but probably won't be able to offer you financial rewards).

Presidential Freedom Scholarships

www.nationalservice.org/scholarships

Learn how to get nominated for a Presidential Freedom Scholarship. Each high school in the country may select up to two students (juniors and seniors only) to receive these $1,000 awards.

City Year

www.cityyear.org

With programs in over a dozen American cities, City Year is rapidly becoming a nationwide organization of people working to improve their communities. Participants work full-time, five days a week, painting, cleaning, teaching, planting, and tutoring. They receive a small stipend and an end-of-the-year education bonus worth $4,725.

Aid for Would-be Health Professionals

National Health Service Corps

nhsc.bhpr.hrsa.gov

Bureau of Health Professions

bhpr.hrsa.gov/nursing/aid.htm

If you are thinking about becoming a doctor or a nurse, you should consider the federal government's programs for health professionals. For example, if you pledge to work in an underserved area, you can get major help in paying for your education from the National Health Service Corps in the form of scholarships and loan repayment.

If You're an Athlete...

Financial aid takes on a whole new meaning if you are an athlete with talent. But before you drool over possible offers, check the following sites to stay on top of the regulations governing athletic scholarships.

Guide for the College-Bound Student-Athlete

www.ncaa.org/eligibility/cbsa

Produced by the National Collegiate Athletic Association, this guide should be read by every high-school athlete who is serious about getting an athletic scholarship. You will find everything from academic-eligibility requirements to information on agents.

The rules about the types of gifts athletes and their families can and cannot accept are very strict. This site is critical to helping you stay within the boundaries.

National Junior College Athletic Association (NJCAA)
www.njcaa.org

If you are thinking about playing sports at a junior college, don't miss this site. It gives information on athletic scholarships and academic-eligibility requirements. It also offers the full text of its publications. (You will need Adobe Acrobat Reader to view the files, however. Most recent computers come with the software, but for information on downloading it, see the instructions on the NJCAA site.)

With three divisions, and over 500 member schools, the NJCAA represents virtually every community college in the country, but you might want to browse the site's directory anyway—just to make sure the school you want is part of the program.

Women's Sports Foundation
www.womenssportsfoundation.org

A wonderful resource for female athletes, as well as those interested in a sports career. You'll find fitness information, current news, and a wealth of grants and scholarships.

Recruitment Services

If you want to spend money (anywhere from $29 - $595) you can hook up with one of these online "recruitment assistance" services. In exchange for your fee, they let you post an athletic profile (and sometimes a 'highlights' video) where it's available to hundreds (or thousands) of college coaches. For an additional fee, some offer personalized service, as well. Of course, there are no guarantees. And many college coaches still prefer to identify new talent in person (at summer sports camps and high school competitions), or rely on referrals from high school coaches. Here are some of your online options, listed from least costly to most expensive:

CollegeRecruiting.com
collegerecruiting.com

Scout USA
www.scoutusa.com

PrepStar
prepstar.com

College Prospects of America
www.cpoa.com

College Partnership
www.collegepartnership.com/athletics.htm

National Directory of College Athletics
www.collegiatedirectories.com

If you opt for self-promotion, rather than a fee-based service, visit this site for e-mail addresses of college coaches in your sport. Then send a polite note, accompanied by a description of your athletic accomplishments, and maybe a link to your own Web site so coaches can learn more, and see you in action.

Commercial Education Loans

If you still need money to help pay the college bills, you might consider a commercial education loan. You can revisit the lenders listed in Chapter 11, or check the following resources. By disclosing your name, address, phone number, social security number, date of birth, income and monthly rent (or mortgage payment), you can usually apply online and learn whether or not you are approved within minutes.

eStudent Loan
www.estudentloan.com

This site (previously mentioned in Chapter 11) lets you compare a half dozen loan programs side-by-side to see which ones offer the best deals. But remember, some of the biggest lenders do not participate in the service, so if you rely exclusively on LoanFinder you may miss the best deal.

Parents pay attention. If you need help paying college bills, there are dozens of commercial education loans from which to choose. Your college, however, may only recommend one or two. It may have worked out a special deal for its students. If not, you can either trust that the college did its homework, and selected the best of the lot, or you can investigate on your own. Use online calculators and compare interest rates (and interest capitalization policy), loan limits, fees, and repayment options. If you're a homeowner, don't forget to compare the options to a home-equity loan. Quite often, you'll find that's your best deal.

The Education Research Institute
www.teri.org

TERI, as it is commonly known, offers loans based on creditworthiness, not income. It provides loans for part-time students, parents, U.S. students in international programs, and more.

Nellie Mae
www.nelliemae.com

The New England Loan Marketing Association (Nellie Mae) is known for private loans; one is EXCEL, which is designed for parents. But it also offers federally guaranteed loans, such as the PLUS Loan for parents of undergraduates and the Stafford Loan.

PLATO
www.plato.org

A student, or any family member, may borrow between $1,000 and $25,000 a year under a PLATO loan (via Wells Fargo Bank). Wells Fargo also offers federally guaranteed loans, and loan-consolidation options. You may apply on line for pre-approval of your creditworthiness.

GATE, or Guaranteed Access to Education
www.gateloan.com

Two loan programs to help with tuition financing: (1) Gate Student Loan Program (through Bank of America) that may be used at over 1500 schools nationwide. (2) College-customized GATE loans that are used by over fifty colleges to supplement financial-aid packages for accepted students. A list of institutions that use GATE is available on this site.

International Education Finance Corporation
www.IEFC.com

The IEFC offers loans to international students studying in the United States AND to U.S. students studying abroad.

Installment Plans

Some schools offer interest-free monthly payment plans that let you spread out your tuition payments. Instead of writing two big checks, one at the start of each semester, you write 10 or 12 smaller ones—a considerable boon to your cash flow. These plans are usually administered by an outside agency. For example:

TuitionPay from Academic Management Services
www.tuitionpay.com

Tuition Management Systems
www.afford.com

A Few More Radical Options ...

eCollegeBid
www.ecollegebid.com

In the era of eBay and Priceline, bidding for goods and services has become more common than ever. Now a group of private colleges has decided that people should be able to bid for college, too. Students and parents who come to this site will have the opportunity to submit a bid for what they would like to pay annually for a college education. The participating colleges—which are schools that admit that they are not "household names"—will take a look at that bid and if they like it, they will get in touch with the bidder to work out the details.

There are a few major drawbacks. For example, few colleges participate in eCollegebid so your "bid" may be going to schools that you otherwise would never have considered. Also, you may wind up paying more for college than if you had applied for aid the old-fashioned way. Many schools discount tuition for students they really want. Would you have received a full-tuition academic award? A talent scholarship? You'll never know.

Sage Tuition Rewards Program
www.student-aid.com

Parents (or grandparents) who invest with Horace Mann Annuities will earn an undergraduate tuition reduction (at participating colleges) equal to 5% of their average annual account balance to a maximum of $15,600 per student, or one year's tuition, whichever is less. Example: A $20,000 balance held for five years would earn a tuition reduction reward of $5,000.

If your child decides not to go to one of the 135 participating colleges, the money you've invested is still yours to use as you choose, and the reward amount may be transferred to another student.

UPromise
www.upromise.com

Shop online at JCrew or Old Navy, Speigel or The Sports Authority, and earn money for college. UPromise has signed up hundreds of partners, including restaurants, credit card companies, and online merchants. Spend money with any of them, and the sponsoring company will put a percentage of your purchase (generally from 2-10%), into a "Section 529" College Savings Plan.

BabyMint
www.babymint.com

BabyMint offers you another way to save for college by shopping, and earning rebates on your purchases. In addition, each dollar you "earn" is matched by a dollar off tuition at nearly 150 colleges and universities across the country.

My Rich Uncle
www.myrichuncle.com

In lieu of a loan, MyRichUncle will advance you the funds you need to pay for college. In turn, you promise to pay MyRichUncle a fixed percentage of your future income, anywhere from 2-15%, for a set period of time (generally 10-15 years). At the end of your agreed-upon repayment period, your obligation is over, regardless of how much you've actually repaid.

PART FIVE

■■■■■■■■■■■■■■■■■

IF YOU'VE PROCRASTINATED
FOR TOO LONG . . .

Annual Student Vacancy Survey

www.nebhe.org/vacancy_survey.html

If you'd like to go to college in the New England area, but wonder if it's too late, visit this site (between May and August) to look through the annual vacancy survey. You may be surprised at how many colleges are still taking applications. Browse for openings at over 200 colleges in Connecticut, Maine, Massachusetts, New Hampshire, Rhode Island, and Vermont.

NACAC Space Availability Survey

www.nacac.com/survey/results.cfm

Each spring, the National Association of College Admission Counselors (NACAC) surveys its members and compiles a list of colleges and universities that have not yet met their fall enrollment goals. And each spring, NACAC posts the results (but don't look for it during the fall and winter). The NACAC survey also gives information on available housing and unclaimed financial aid.

If you have trouble accessing the site, you may also request a copy of the results by calling NACAC's fax-on-demand, (703) 299-6829.

PART SIX

■■■■■■■■■■■■■■■■■

Cyber-College Life

CHAPTER 13

■■■■■■■■■■■■■■■■■■■■■■

THE FUN STUFF

You've finished! The search process is over, the SAT is history, the admission applications are sitting in some dean's office waiting to be reviewed, and the financial-aid applications are in the mail. It's time to sit back, relax, and dream of what college will be like.

Or maybe you are just taking a break. Either way, here are a few fun spots, listed alphabetically, to give you a glimpse of cyber-college life.

#1 Free Stuff
www.1freestuff.com

Start practicing for your starving-student days by checking out all the fun things you can get for free!

The Black Collegian Online
www.black-collegian.com

Get a monthly dose of information about post-college career opportunities. Here you'll also find commentary by leading African-American writers, entertainment features, and general information on college life.

Campus Access
www.campusaccess.com

Although it was designed for Canadian college students, this site is brimming with information that can help any first-year student, anywhere. Read essays about how to get prepared for independence, how to choose a major, how to take notes, and how to survive if you can't stand your roommates.

College Club
www.collegeclub.com

The folks at College Club have pumped up their site—adding e-mail and instant message services, 24-hour chat rooms, interactive polls, online forums, discount directories, personal home pages, Web cams, you name it. College students (and college-bound students, too) may register for free.

mtvU

www.mtvu.com

Owned by MTV, mtvU plays a mix of music ranging from hip hop to rock. It also also sponsors a variety of contests and features segments on everyday campus life—food, fashion, sports, travel, and more.

 If you're using a slow machine, beware. Most of these sites are graphics-heavy. And if you turn off the images function on your browser, some of what makes these fun will disappear.

Colleges.com

www.colleges.com

Search for scholarships, test yourself with textbook quizzes and read through issues of U.Magazine, a tabloid that is distributed on campuses.

CampusEstore.com

www.campusestore.com

Get discounts on computer equipment, software, electronics and more. These discounts are only available to college students. But if you are a high-school senior who has been accepted to college, you too can participate. To get in, you must send a copy of your acceptance letter.

GreekPages

www.greekpages.com

Here's the place to get a sense of what fraternity and sorority members around the country are talking about. The site, which is updated regularly, also provides links to "hellenistic" chapters with innovative Web sites.

GreekSource

www.greeksource.com

This site has become dedicated to message boards and chat. Don't bother checking in if you have an ancient Web browser—the sites use the latest java technology.

The Internet Guide to Spring Break

www.springbreak.com

Dreaming of a sun-baked week with your new college buddies? Check out this site during the spring break season (March and April) to see live beach Web cams of hot spots. Until then, find out about last year's "kewl" destinations, and take a peek at yearbooks of previous spring breaks.

Pick-a-Prof

www.pick-a-prof.com

Start studying up on your future professors. Pick-a-Prof is still expanding, but if your school is included, you can get an advance peek at a professor's lecture style, attendance policy, grading history, and more. The reviews are written by students; the grade distributions are compiled directly from university records (thanks to state open record laws).

Roommate Service.Com

www.roommates.com

If you plan to live off-campus, this site, with over 150,000 listings, can help you find the perfect roommate.

StudentAdvantage.Com

www.studentadvantage.com

Works with thousands of merchants to develop (and sell) products for students in categories ranging from dorm decor to wireless and telecom.

Student.Com

www.student.com

Student.com serves up sassy articles on campus culture, jobs and travel. Also relationship advice, personal ads, and links to hundreds of student diaries.

Student Counseing Virtual Pamphlet Collection

counseling.uchicago.edu/vpc/virtulets.html

This site links to hundreds of virtual pamphlets published by an assortment of university counseling centers. Topics include alcohol and substance abuse, sexual harassment, study skills, test-taking and time management.

The Universal Black Pages

www.ubp.com

Link into a bunch of educational information, including home pages of historically black colleges, African-American student groups, fraternities, and sororities. The site contains links to non-college resources too.

For more e-zines, try the lists at Yahoo! or Google

dir.yahoo.com/News_and_Media/College_and_University/Magazines

directory.google.com/Top/News/Colleges_and_Universities/
Magazines_and_E-zines

CHAPTER 14

■■■■■■■■■■■■■■■■■■■■

E-CAMPUS BOOKSTORES
AND ONLINE LECTURE NOTES

On line or In line?

Online book buying is becoming a popular replacement for waiting in line with arms aching from baskets of heavy books.

Most freshmen wait until they arrive on campus before buying their textbooks—and experiencing sticker shock. But the Web can give you a head start. If you already know your classes, head to Amazon or Barnes & Noble online, or a textbook-oriented e-bookseller with your credit card (or, more likely, your parents' credit card) ready. You can save up to 40 percent on the cost of new books, and, sometimes, have them delivered for free. Many bookselling sites offer other college-related merchandise too—so check their prices before you head out for a back-to-school spree.

If you want to play it safe and wait until school starts, you should still take a look at these e-booksellers and familiarize yourself with how they work—in addition to discounts on new books, they usually offer a large selection of used textbooks, as well as book buybacks and discounts for referring your book-buying friends. And, if you're still trying to decide between courses, peeking at reading lists can help you make your decision.

Best Book Buys
www.bestbookbuys.com

To use this nifty site, simply enter a book's title, author, keyword or ISBN. BestBookBuys then searches through 27 different online bookstores and displays the price, availability, shipping method and shipping charges at each. For example, total costs for a new copy of Marilyn Stokstad's *Art History* (2nd ed., revised) ranged from $71 to $99.

EFollett

www.Efollet.com

Follett has been a family-owned business for over 12 years and manages hundreds of college bookstores across the country. EFollet joins 1,000 of those bookstores in an e-partnership. Follet's Internet site organizes book lists by college, and offers both new and used texts. Follet will ship books to you (for a fee), or, you can arrange to pick up your order on-campus.

VarsityBooks.com

www.varsitybooks.com

New and used textbooks. You can search by title, author or ISBN.

Big Words

www.bigwords.com

Like BestBookBuys, this site searches online stores and returns a list of book options for you to pursue. It also features a book buy-back option.

E Campus

www.ecampus.com

Another e-bookstore; this one has a lucrative buy-back program. Just enter your book's ISBN and learn the buy-back price; sometimes you'll get as much as 50% of the purchase price. ECampus also offers online auctions and special deals on computers, clothes and DVDs.

ClassBook.com

www.classbook.com

Another site to buy and sell new and used textbooks.

Publishers assign every edition of every book a unique ten-digit ISBN ("International Standard Book Number"). You'll find this identifying number on the book's back cover (as part of the bar code), or on an inside page, with the copyright information.

DORM Store

www.dormtours.net/eshop.asp

Take a virtual tour of actual college dorm rooms, so you know what to expect, then go e-shopping to recreate the coolest looks. This site also lets you "register" for stuff, in case your friends and relatives want to give you a going-away-to-college present.

Class Notes On the Web

Don't want to go to class? No problem. Sleep in, then download the day's lecture notes from the comfort of your dorm room. That is the pitch of a new breed of sites which provide class notes, free of charge, via the Web.

Lecture note sites employ students from across the country to post class notes to their specific area of the site. The 'guides' or 'tutors' maintain their area with up-to-date reports on class meetings, topic-driven chats, and even host study sessions before exams.

Do commercial sites have the right to publish class notes? Legal issues over intellectual property are now playing out in the courts, and the main "class notes" sites from previous editions of *College.edu* have disappeared into thin cyber-air. Some universities, like MIT and Penn State, however, have simply decided to beat these companies at their own game, and distribute their own course lecture notes (freely) on the Web.

MIT's OpenCourseWare
ocw.mit.edu

The Massachusetts Institute of Technology has committed $100 million to OpenCourseWare, and will go online with lecture notes, course outlines, reading lists and homework assignments for all 2,000 of its courses over the next 10 years (700 courses are already available). This site is completely free of charge, so anyone in the world can benefit from an MIT education, minus the classroom interaction between faculty and student (which MIT notes is the "fundamental cornerstone" of its learning process).

YourNotes
www.yournotes.com

Founded by students from Penn State, YourNotes includes lecture notes from Penn State courses only.

Cheater-Catchers

While the Web has made it easier to access contraband educational material, it has also added new weapons to the arsenals of teachers trying to curb plagiarism. Several sites let teachers match text strings that 'seem suspicious' to documents that are available online. They simply enter a sentence or two from a student's paper and find out if the exact or similar phrase appears somewhere on the Web. It is then up to the professor to visit the site and judge whether the passage in question is indeed plagiarized, or simply cut from a similar idea.

The mere existence of these paper-matching sites is enough to keep most students from purchasing papers online.

Plagiarism.org

www.plagiarism.org

Chief among these sites is Plagiarism.org which compares provided text with millions of web pages and the archives of dozens of free term paper sites.

Turnitin.com

www.turnitin.com

Turn It In works in a similar fashion. Its "Originality Reports" include an "overall similarity index" and color-coded links to contested passages.

Essay Verification Engine (EVE)

www.canexus.com/eve

This low-cost download ($20/user) "reads" essays in plain text, Microsoft Word, or Corel Word Perfect and returns links to web pages from which a student may have plagiarized. If it finds evidence of plagiarism, the URL is recorded. Once the search has completed, the teacher is given a full report on each paper that contained plagiarism, including the percent of the essay plagiarized, and an annotated copy of the paper showing all plagiarism highlighted in red. (And "yes," we "plagiarized" this description from the company's Web site.)

—this section of *College.Edu* was originally prepared
with assistance from Katherine Williamson

APPENDICES

Metasites, FAQs and Indices

APPENDIX 1

■■■■■■■■■■■■■■■■■■■■■

METASITES

These sites attempt to be all things to all people. They have advice for parents and students, tips on choosing and applying, resources on financial aid, college essays, you name it. I call them metasites, and depending on your personality or the information you are looking for, they just might become your favorite stop on the Internet. They are arranged in alphabetical order, so their placement does not reflect quality. If a site seems to have gaps or disadvantages, you'll see that noted.

@theU
www.attheu.com

A site for the student shopper—with a bonus: You earn "UniBucks" worth up to 5% of every purchase made on the site. Once you've earned $25 worth of UniBucks, @theU will apply that money to your student loan account, reducing the amount you will need to repay. That means you have to spend at least $500 at this Web site's campus store—not an easy task, unless you buy all your text books here. But even to browse the bookstore, you must sign up for an account and divulge your e-mail address.

About.Com's College Admissions page
collegeapps.about.com

A section devoted to information for college-bound students and their parents. Read about everything from scholarship myths and misconceptions to distance-learning programs.

> Most of these sites require you to "sign in" or "register" before you can peek inside (or at least get to the good stuff). By disclosing this information, you are helping the site show its advertisers that people of your demographic profile are clicking around. You're also giving it useful information for marketers and advertisers. Neither of which is necessarily bad—but you should know how these sites work.

America Online's College Prep area

In AOL, go to keyword "college," and you'll find a bunch of stuff on financial aid, links to articles and Web sites that help narrow your search, plus useful links for the college bound.

Black Excel
www.blackexcel.org

Read about historically black colleges, learn about the black greek experience, and browse through the directory of black student unions at colleges across the country. The site also offers admissions advice and a gateway to scholarship services.

College Board Online
www.collegeboard.com

Take some time to dig through all the material. You'll find a guide to campus visits, columns about what admission officers look for in applicants, financial-aid calculators, and online registration for the SAT. There is also a section for education professionals, including high-school counselors.

The College Guide
www.mycollegeguide.org

Brought to you by FishNet, this site lets you search for a college, ask questions of the admission guru, download the common application, or browse the "money for college" section. Updated monthly.

CollegeNET
www.collegenet.com

Includes MACH25, the scholarship search described in Chapter 12. Also offers electronic applications for hundreds of schools, a database of college information, links to financial-aid hot spots, and some virtual tours.

College Planning
www.collegeplan.org

A fantastic resource for students living in the Pacific Northwest—and a still-valuable site for students living elsewhere. Search the scholarship guide, read the keys to college selection and admission, and take a walk through the "money maze."

CollegePrep 101

collegeprep.okstate.edu/

This site was developed by the College of Education at Oklahoma State University. It includes everything from college terminology to recruitment materials to stress management to what's trendy on campuses today.

CollegeView

www.collegeview.com

A good source for virtual tours of college campuses—if you have the power PC and speedy Internet connection to handle the fancy graphics. The site, published by Hobsons Publishing, also offers a database of information searchable by college, with the option to "zap" quick e-mail inquiries to the colleges of your choice.

CollegeXpress

www.collegexpress.com

A colorful site built primarily as a gateway to information on private colleges. But it's stocked with tools for anyone, including a college search, scholarship search and loan search, as well as admission and financial aid advice and a parents' corner.

EduPrep

www.eduprep.com

This site has a simple slogan—Get Ready for College. You'll find college admissions help, test prep, college tours, a scholarship search, student loans, and an essay writing course.

FinAid Page

www.finaid.org

A one-stop shop for information about student loans, federal programs, scholarship services, and more. This resource can't be beat. Compiled and updated by Mark Kantrowitz, a Web publisher and financial-aid expert.

Go College

www.gocollege.com

College and scholarship searches, expert advice, practice tests, distance learning, campus bookstore and campus entertainment.

Guidance On-Line

home.cfl.rr.com/nwunder/guidance.html

A useful list of links to college search pages, financial-aid sites, scholarship data bases, and more. Updated regularly by Olympia High School in Orlando, Florida.

MyRoad.com

www.myroad.com

This site, acquired by The College Board, offers something many of the others don't: advice for students who first want to figure out their career paths and then choose a college based on those plans. The only drawback? It ain't free. In fact, it will cost you $19.95 a year if your high school doesn't have a deal with MyRoad. If you decide to pay for it, the site also provides a searchable database of colleges as well as information about the job market.

Peterson's Education Portal

www.petersons.com

Brought to you by Peterson's, the long-time publisher of college guides. This well-designed site includes news and announcements, test prep, college search services, online applications, financial aid and scholarship data, and—of course—promos for Peterson's books.

Princeton Review

www.princetonreview.com

In addition to test-prep, this site (which has recently combined with Embark.com) offers online applications, a scholarship search, and a database of college information. Also provides career advice and tells students what to pack for college. The site's forums are one of its most interesting features, with postings from hundreds of students.

ScholarStuff

www.scholarstuff.com

This site does not provide much original content, but it does a decent job collecting hundreds of useful links to college-related sites on the Web. It's also a good stop for links to international universities and information on sororities and fraternities.

WiredScholar
www.wiredscholar.com

Sponsored by student-loan behemoth Sallie Mae, Wired Scholar has folders on preparing, selecting, applying and paying for college, as well as interactive tools to help you evaluate your financial-aid award letters and make your final college decision. This site will soon be changing its name and address to "CollegeAnswer.com"

■ ■ ■ ■ ■ ■ ■ ■ ■ ■ ■ ■ ■ ■

THINKING AHEAD:
GETTING READY FOR GRADUATE SCHOOL

College.edu focuses on college planning for undergraduates; however, there are numerous web sites that will help you get ready for graduate school as well. Meta-sites for Med School, Law School and Business School are especially plentiful, so if you think there's an MCAT, LSAT or GMAT in your future, here's a site sampler to get you started.

Student Doctor Network
www.studentdoctor.net

This site contains useful information for medical students, dental students and allied health students. You'll find advice on getting in (and getting through) med school, financial aid information, residency listings, and health care career information. You can also read medical student diaries and participate in forums and chat rooms. And, you can navigate through over 1000 links, including e-books, health care humor and sites for pre-med students.

FindLaw for Students
stu.findlaw.com/prelaw

Lots of articles, on lots on useful topics—Considering Law School, Financing Law School, Law School Admission Information, Law School Rankings, Pre-Law Discussion Forums, Pre-Law Organizations and Preparing for Law School.

Internet Legal Resource Guide
www.ilrg.com/pre-law.html

Brought to you by current students at The University of Texas School of Law, this site will link you up with a variety of pre-law services, like LSAT preparation, pre-law advising programs, first year prep courses, and dozens of law school rankings.

Law Students

www.law.com/jsp/students.jsp

Interesting news articles as well as law school rankings, bar exam preparation and career information.

MBA.com

www.mba.com

The Graduate Management Admission Council has developed this search engine to help you choose the right MBA program for you. This site will also help you prepare for the GMAT, link up with financial aid possibilities, and develop effective job search strategies.

APPENDIX 2

■■■■■■■■■■■■■■■■■■■■■■■■

FAQS FOR INTERNET NEWBIES
(FREQUENTLY ASKED QUESTIONS
FOR INTERNET NEWCOMERS)

Feeling left behind? Still unsure what people mean when they talk about bookmarks, browsers, and bad links? The following questions and answers should help you catch up. For those who already understand Internet basics, skip ahead. Some answers at the end—such as how plug-ins work— just might teach you something you don't yet know.

What is the Internet?

The Internet is one enormous INTERNATIONAL NETWORK of computers that can communicate with each other. Some are connected by MODEMS, which are machines that make connections using telephone lines. (This is the case for most people who use the Internet at home.) Many are linked by high-speed lines and cables, which allow much faster communication. And a few are connected via satellites.

The communication that occurs on this enormous network can take many forms. Electronic mail, or E-MAIL, is one of the simplest forms. In e-mail, a single message is sent from one computer to another. Newsgroups and the World Wide Web are more complex.

What are newsgroups? Usenet?

Newsgroups are the Internet's community kiosks. USENET (a huge 'user's network') links most of them together. People post hundreds of announce- ments, questions, and pieces of advice in some 50,000 newsgroups each day. Most material posted in newsgroups is junk—but you never know when something helpful might turn up.

Newsgroups started before the days of the Web, so you can access them with "newsreader" software available on many of the computers used in university computer labs. If you don't have newsreader software, the easiest way to browse through newsgroups is via your Internet browser, or Google at groups.google.com. Google lets you search the entire newsgroup system for one "article" or post, or search for a specific newsgroup topic. (For more on newsgroups, see Chapter 1.)

What is the World Wide Web?

The Web is a subset of the Internet made up of picture, sound, and text files located on computers around the world that can be viewed by people on other computers around the world. The Web brought the Internet alive by giving it color, images, and easy-to-use commands.

What is HTML?

For a file to be "viewable" on the Web, it must be coded using HTML, or hypertext markup language. HTML can be read by any Web browser—regardless of whether the computer is a Macintosh, Windows-based PC, or Unix machine.

What is a URL?

Universal Resource Locator. This is cyberlingo for the path or address of a particular site. URLs on the Web usually look something like this: www.site.com/lookhere.html

What does http://www.site.com/lookhere.html mean?

"http" signifies the material is available on the Web. "www.site.com" is called the domain name. Think of it as the storage center for the files you're viewing. The rest of the address, in this case "lookhere.html," tells your Web browser exactly which files to display from that storage area.

What do ".com," ".edu," ".gov" ".org" and ".mil" mean?

These domains denote whether a site is run by a commercial company (.com), an institution of higher education (.edu), a government site (.gov), a non-profit organization (.org) or the military (.mil). Outside the United States, names end in abbreviations for the country, such as .ca for Canada.

The domain '.edu' is usually a reliable indicator—most Web sites with '.edu' suffixes are in fact universities or colleges. But some not-so-kosher companies will assign themselves a '.edu' suffix even though they are not non-profits, are not accredited, and are not institutions of higher learning. Until domain names are better regulated, Net surfers should never assume a Web site is legitimate simply because it uses '.edu' in its address.

What is a Web browser?

Netscape Navigator and Microsoft Internet Explorer are Web browsers. There are other less common ones as well. Web browsers are instruments for viewing HTML files. All browsers contain a field where a person can enter the path, or URL, for a Web page. Once the path is entered, the browser displays its contents in the window below. Browsers also contain a "status bar" to show you the address of your current URL; scroll bars to help you move up and down pages more quickly; "back" and "forward" buttons to let you move back and forth between sites you've already visited; a "favorite" or "bookmark" icon to help you add and organize your favorite sites; and a "stop" button to interrupt file transfers (very useful when you get tired of waiting for a slow file to load).

What is a home page?

Generally, a home page is a file that stakes out a person's or organization's place on the Web. A university's home page is the front page of its Web site, which could contain hundreds of interior pages.

What is hypertext?

When using the Web, you will see words that are highlighted in color and underlined. These are the most common form of hyperlinks. When you click on hyperlinks and arrive at new pages with more hyperlinked words, you are experiencing hypertext. It is a nonlinear way of reading texts and examining images, in which a person can find out what is "behind" the word simply by clicking on it.

Why do some sites take so long to load?

The Internet's speed is usually based on four major factors: 1) the speed of the connection from your computer to the outside world, 2) the volume of traffic on the Internet, 3) the amount of material you are trying to transmit, and 4) the speed of the connection on the computer holding the files you are trying to view.

If you are using a computer that connects to the Internet without a modem—for example, one with a high speed line like a T1 line or an **ISDN** (Integrated Services Digital Network) line—you will find that pages load much more quickly. Theoretically, the speed can be hundreds of times faster than with a 28.8 Kbps modem (see below). Since T1 lines and ISDN connections still cost quite a bit more money than simple modems, they are most commonly found in places with heavy Internet usage, such as your high school, your parents' office, or your local library. However, you may be fortunate enough to live in an area that provides cable or DSL (digital subscriber line) access where Internet connections at home are just as fast as in the office.

If you are using a MODEM, you will often have to wait for pages to load—especially if the site contains a lot of hefty material, such as photographs, animated pictures, and large text files. On a 14.4 Kbps modem (one that runs at a speed of 14,400 bits per second) you will be often be waiting a long time. Modems with 28.8, 33.6, and 56K speeds are faster—but still no dynamos. BITS, by the way, are the smallest pieces of information that can be sent between computers.

So what can I do about it?

Here are a few tricks to help you avoid traffic jams on the supposedly speedy information super highway:

Most Web browsers give you the option of NOT loading images. This means you will only be able to view text. Where images should be you'll see what are called "BROKEN GRAPHICS," which are the symbols for image files that do not show up properly on your browser. Well-designed Web sites will provide alternative text as replacements for broken graphics so that you may still get a sense of what is being shown on the page.

To take advantage of this option, you'll have to change your "preferences" or preferred settings. In Netscape Navigator, you'll find these settings by pulling down the "edit" menu, choosing "preferences," and then "advanced" settings. From there you can un-check the box labeled "automatically upload images." On Internet Explorer, pull down the "tools" menu, select "Internet options" and go to the "advanced" area. You'll find the box labeled "show pictures" under the heading "multimedia."

Also, advanced browsers allow you to decide whether you want to receive the images during or after the text of the page has loaded. Select the "after" option so that you will be able to read the page while the computer cranks out the graphics.

Finally, you may want to be selective about when you get on line. Avoid Internet rush hours, such as weekday evenings and weekend afternoons. Avoid big news days, like election day, when the Internet will be clogged with too many users as well.

What are bookmarks? How do I save them from one computer to another?

Bookmarks got their name from Netscape; other brands use words like Internet Explorer's "Favorites" or AOL's "Favorite Places." These are handy lists of sites you have seen once and want to visit again.

When you "bookmark" a page, you are saving the address to a file on your hard drive. Your bookmarks, therefore, are not very portable—unless you set your browser to save them on a disk instead. Under the word "bookmarks" on Netscape, click on "go to bookmarks" or "edit bookmarks." Under the file menu, you'll see a "save as" option, which will allow you to save the bookmarks to a diskette or a networked drive. Most other browsers give you the same option.

When you go to another computer and want to use these bookmarks, pop in your disk, open "go to bookmarks" or "edit bookmarks" and choose "open" under the file menu. You'll then be able to retrieve them from the A: drive.

To organize your slew of bookmarked sites, use your Web browser to set up folders according to categories you design. For example, you might want one folder for your list of favorite colleges, another for your materials on financial aid, and a third for all the fun stuff in Chapter 13.

How does e-mail work on the Web?

Most people use e-mail on an online service like America Online or on a local Internet service provider. (The latest versions of Netscape and Internet Explorer provide their own e-mail services, as do many Web sites.) But sometimes a Web page will provide a HYPERTEXT LINK TO AN E-MAIL ADDRESS. When you click on that address, a window will open in which you can type a message and hit send.

If you are on a computer at home, feel free to use this option. If it is your first time using e-mail on Netscape, for example, you will often get a message asking you to set your return e-mail address. To do that, follow the directions given, which differ depending on the browser you are using.

But if you are on someone else's computer—such as the one in your high-school library—avoid using Web-based e-mail. If you see a link to an e-mail address, write the address down and use it later, when you are on your own e-mail system. Sending a message from someone else's computer means the return address is also someone else's. If the person receiving your e-mail hits the "reply" button, he or she will be replying to that e-mail address instead of yours. (Some administrators have "locked" the e-mail mechanism on public computers so this won't happen—but you can never be too sure.)

Here's a tip: Always write your e-mail address after your name when you send e-mail. That way, if the message is ever truncated or forwarded, the recipient will still have an address for you.

Some e-mail programs let you create "signature files" which automatically attach to the end of each e-mail message (or newsgroup posting). You can use this "sig" for all your contact information, like your full name, mailing address, e-mail address, phone number, and high school name. Keep it under five lines, and avoid including "meaningful" quotes, or unnecessary personal data.

In choosing your e-mail name, use your real name (or your first initial and last name). Admission officers won't be impressed by a letter from someone named Bob2Cool or KittyKat.

How about free e-mail services?

If you do not have your own Web connection, you can sign up for a free e-mail account with BigFoot (www.bigfoot.com) , CollegeClub (www.collegeclub.com), HotMail (hotmail.com), Lycos (comm.lycos.com), or Mail.com (www.mail.com), as well as with most large search engines like Yahoo. Your messages will be stored on the sponsoring company's server, not your own, so you can easily check your e-mail from any computer with an Internet connection.

There are several other advantages to setting up a free e-mail account (even if you do have your own computer). First, you can use this name when you register with all the college search sites. This should reduce the amount of junk e-mail that finds its way into your "real" account. Second, if you absolutely must have a funky online moniker, you can use free accounts to change your persona every week. Third, if you plan to visit chat rooms, you can use your alternate name. Again, this should help limit the junk e-mail that would otherwise clog up your regular mail box.

On the downside, free e-mail accounts come with lots of advertisements (which is why they are "free"), and they can be quite slow.

If I don't use one of these free e-mail services, how can I check my e-mail when I'm away from my home?

Assuming you have a computer with Internet access, Mail2Web makes it simple to tap into your ISP and retrieve your e-mail. Just log onto www.mail2web.com, enter your e-mail address (or IP Address) and password, and this utility does the rest. It now supports AOL email as well.

If you are accessing from your PDA, use www.mail2pda.com; if you have a WAP (wireless application protocol) compatible mobile phone, dial www.mail2wap.com.

How can I make sure my e-mail is private?

When you send an e-mail message, you are sending the equivalent of a postcard. If that message is ever intercepted, it can be read by anyone who happens to pick it up. So if you are sending something confidential or if you have a touch of paranoia, you may want to check out the latest private e-mail services. A company called ZixMail, for example, offers the equivalent of locked envelopes in which you may transport your messages (www.zixmail.com). It requires downloadable software and costs $50 a year, but it will work with almost any mail system including AOL.

Two other services are ZipLip.com and HushMail.com.

What are viruses, and how do I avoid them?

Viruses are nasty, replicable programs that can infect your computer's hard drive. Viruses can be minor nuisances that change the way a particular program runs or they can corrupt your entire operating system.

If you use virus-scanning software like that offered by Symantec or McAfree, you can usually rest assured that you aren't unknowingly bringing viruses into your computer. Most computers at schools and libraries have this type of "disinfectant" to ward off viruses.

If you don't know whether the computer you are using has virus-checking software, you might want to refrain from putting anything unknown onto your hard drive. Viruses can only get to your hard drive if they have access to it—so if you never download anything or insert any unknown diskettes into your computer, you should be fine.

You cannot catch viruses from e-mail messages or Web-surfing, unless you download an infected file. The ILOVEYOU virus that gained popularity was an "attachment" to an E-mail message. It could only be activated by being opened, which is typically done by clicking on the attachment icon that comes in the e-mail message. Never click on an attached file unless you know what it is and why it was sent to you.

To avoid viruses on diskettes, use only those that have been inserted into computers you are familiar with. Nearly all the plug-ins and other downloadable files noted in this book have been secured by Web site owners to ensure that they are safe from viruses.

Where do America Online and Microsoft Network fit in?

These are nationwide, commercial providers of Internet services. In addition to connecting you to the Internet complete with your own e-mail addresses, they provide their own content—which is available only to those who have signed up with their network.

What are search engines? Where do I find them?

Search engines are the Web's saving grace. For example if you are looking for a site on college football but you don't have a specific URL, go to a search engine like Yahoo!, Google or others, and type the words "college football." The search engine will point you to related sites.

Search engines aren't perfect however—not by a long shot. Some Web sites never turn up in an Internet search, while others pop up all the time—even though their links haven't worked for months. And some Web sites pop up all the time, even though they aren't what you are looking for, because the site's designer has manipulated the system to rise to the top.

So to get the most out of your search engine, you should know some basics about how they work. First, learn the difference between a **raw search** of the Web, which pulls up links to anything out there, and a search of an **already-compiled directory** of Web sites reviewed by human beings. If you are looking for something obscure, you probably want to search the entire Web. If you want something more common, like "college football," then you will have the most luck with an already-compiled directory.

Fortunately, the most popular search services now allow you to do both. Here are some examples.

www.google.com

No frills. Very fast. You can search the entire Web, or look through specific categories, images, or pdf files. And you seldom come across bad addresses, since Google takes a snapshot of every page it examines and stores it as a "cached" link. In other words, if the page you're looking for is currently unavailable, you can view it as it last appeared to Google. FYI: Googol equals the number "1" followed by 100 zeroes.

If you're a frequent Google user, you can save yourself time by installing the Google toolbar—at toolbar.google.com—and using it to do searches without having to always go to the Google homepage.

www.yahoo.com

Categorizes hundreds of thousands of Web sites—and if those sites don't provide what you want, Yahoo automatically switches to Google to search the entire Web. Yahoo was one of the first search services on the Web and to this day it is the most popular.

www.alltheweb.com

This search engine has a refreshing inclination to find non-American pages—a byproduct of its Norwegian roots. In fact, you can search in

49 different languages. It's also got a huge index—sometimes challenging Google in size.

www.teoma.com

Teoma (which means "expert" in Gaelic) prides itself on implementing a new method for pulling up pages that match your chosen keywords. While Google looks for pages that contain keywords *and* are deemed worthy by authoritative web sites, Teoma looks for pages within specialized niches and *then* applies Google's strategy. Reviewers are not entirely convinced that this new approach works as well as Teoma's engineers think, but again, it is worth a try if you are combing the Web for hard-to-find pages. Teoma is now owned by "Ask Jeeves."

www.altavista.com

More browsable directories plus full-Web searches, multimedia searches, and tools like e-mail, radio and the yellow pages. Also includes Babel Fish Translation, a feature that instantly translates websites (or plain text) from one language into another. Very Quickly.

As the Web expands, search engines are less and less helpful for non-specific searches. If you type a single common word like "college" or "scholarship," you'll end up with tens of thousands of sites to visit—clearly, a daunting journey.

AOL Search

AOL's search service allows you to search for information inside AOL and out on the Web—simultaneously. Go to keyword "search" to use it, and become adept at clicking among "Recommended Sites" and "Matching Sites." AOL Search is now enhanced by Google.

search.msn.com

MSN revamped its search engine in 2004, opting for the streamlined look à la Google.

www.lycos.com

A hub for searching the Web and browsing categories. Includes news, multimedia searching, and parental controls.

search.netscape.com

Netscape uses a directory system called "The Open Directory." It's a competitor to Yahoo that sprung up after Webmasters became fed up with waiting for Yahoo to include their sites. The site also uses a Google search engine for full-Web searches.

Meta-Search Engines

If you're looking for something really obscure, you may want to use several search engines at one time. Fortunately Meta-search engines make that possible. They run searches on multiple search engines at one time, and bring you the results. Here are the ones I have the most luck with:

www.dogpile.com

"Fetches" results by more than a dozen different search engines — and includes several other features to boot. You can search news wires and Usenet, yellow pages, white pages, online auctions, and MP3 files. For regional searches, try Dogpile's geographically-tailored search service. And if you simply want a browsable catalog of sites, Dogpile offers that, too.

www.mamma.com

"The mother of all search engines." This new meta search provides results quickly, and tells you which search engine was used to find the answer.

www.search.com

Brought to you by CNet, an online source of product reviews and technology news.

www.metacrawler.com

This metasearch allows you to customize your search screen by specifying whether you want to search specific domains, like the .edu domain, and lets you select the search engines that you would like to use simultaneously.

How can I get better search results?

Think about what you are searching for. Are you looking for Web sites that relate to commonly understood and broad topics, like shopping or travel? If so, try the human-compiled directories like Yahoo. If you are looking for something very specific, like a rare surname, try a pure search engine that canvasses the entire Web, like Google or a metasearch service like DogPile.

It may also help to brush up on "boolean logic," a search language named for 19th century mathematician George Boole who first reduced logical reasoning to mathematical formulas.

Many search engines work most efficiently when you search using BOOLEAN operators. Don't worry, this is less complicated than it sounds. You just need to become comfortable with using 'and' to combine words, 'or' to split them, quotation marks to search whole phrases, and parentheses to make your search more sophisticated. Here are some examples:

- botany and Indiana: This will bring up all entries that contain both the words botany and Indiana. Use this if you're looking only for Indiana colleges with botany majors.

- botany or Indiana: This will bring up all entries that contain either the word botany or the word Indiana. Use this if you're looking for any college with a botany major, or any college in Indiana.

- botany and (Indiana or Michigan): This will bring up all entries that contain the words botany with the word Indiana or with the word Michigan. Use this if you're looking for schools in either Indiana or Michigan that offer botany majors.

- "field hockey": This will bring up all entries that contain the words field and hockey next to each other, and in that order (instead of looking for the word 'field' in some places and 'hockey' in others). Use this if you're looking for all schools with field hockey teams.

- "field hockey" and (Indiana or Michigan): This will bring up all entries that contain the words "field hockey" with the word Indiana or with the word Michigan. Use this if you're looking only for schools in Indiana or Michigan with field hockey teams.

How do I search a page full of text?

If you are on a page full of text and you are looking for a specific word, pull down the "edit" menu on your browser. Click on "find" and a window will open where you may type in your word. (If you are using Windows, try Control-F.) Hit enter and the browser will find the word on that page and highlight it for you. Unfortunately, more and more Web pages are using new organizing tools, like frames and scroll bars, that often prevent you from searching everything in an entire Web page at one time. But for Web pages that long documents of text, word searching is still a good option.

I clicked on a link that doesn't work. Why is that?

If you click on a hyperlink and get an error message, several different things may be happening—none of which you can really control.

- First, the person who constructed the site might have accidentally introduced a typo into the URL. Your browser, then, is searching for a link that doesn't exist and will tell you so. If this happens, your only recourse is to send a message to the site administrator (often known as a Webmaster), alerting him or her of the problem, and hope that it is corrected soon.

- Second, the site behind the link might have moved. This means the code for that particular link is outdated and needs to be corrected with the new URL. Again, there is no easy way out of these dead ends. One suggestion is to delete everything in the address except for the domain name. In other words, if the URL is www.site.com/lookhere1/lookhere2.html, the specific path may have changed. Go to www.site.com and look through the site index. If that doesn't work, send a message about the problem to the site's Webmaster.

- Third, the site's server may be down. In basic terms, this means the computer that holds all the site's files has lost its connection to the Internet. There is nothing you can do about this except try again later.

- And last, the Internet just might be very busy, making all connections sluggish. Connecting to sites in different countries can take a long time as well. If you don't have the patience to wait for a site to load—and I don't blame you—hit the "STOP" BUTTON on your browser and try a different URL.

My browser continues to reload the same old page, even though I've asked for a new one.

This happens on old browsers often—and is probably because your CACHE is full. What is a cache? It's an area on your hard drive that saves copies of the pages and graphics you have loaded onto your browser. That way, when you return to a page you have already visited, the browser does not have to point all the way back to the site to find the page. It can simply retrieve it from your hard drive.

But that cache can fill up. And when it does, the browser gets confused and fails to retrieve new pages for you. To fix the problem, go to the "options" menu on your browser and ask it to empty the cache (On AOL, go to keyword Preferences, then click on WWW Preferences).

What are plug-ins? Where do I get them?

Plug-ins are utilities that can be added—or "plugged" in—to your browser, enabling it to display many file types beyond simple HTML-coded pages. To see VIDEO, listen to SOUND, and DOWNLOAD software, you usually need a plug-in. The latest browsers have popular plug-ins already installed, so you don't have to do anything. But if you have come across a Web site that requires a plug-in that is not found on your computer, you may need to jump through the hoops to install it.

Installing plug-ins becomes easier after you've done a few, but in the beginning, the process can be harrowing. Since you're adding new software to your computer, you will need to make sure your machine has enough memory to handle the plug-in. You will also be working within the directory of your computer, which is called the "file manager" in early Windows operating systems and "Windows Explorer" in Windows 95, 98 and 2000. On Macs, using plug-ins is less of a hassle, because the desktop is equipped to graphically show you where files are going. When you come to a Web site that requires a plug-in, you will get a message telling you that you will need to install one. Usually, the site will point you to a page that contains links to the one you need. Follow the directions carefully, and for safety's sake, save and close all the files you might be working on at the time.

The plug-in will usually be saved to a temporary folder in your computer. Most advanced browsers automatically take note that the plug-in has been installed, but you will need to shut down and restart the browser to use it.

What does "download" mean? How do I do it?

When you are downloading a file or piece of software, you are saving that file or software to your hard drive. The plug-ins described above have been downloaded from sites on the Web.

Many electronic applications for college-bound students must be down-loaded before they can be used. When you come to a page that asks you to download a file, be prepared to save all your work and reboot your computer. Also, be prepared to wait a while. Depending on the size of the downloadable file, this process can take anywhere from a few minutes to a few hours. Be aware of what your computer can handle. Most electronic applications, fortunately, are not so huge that they require much waiting. Games and videos, however, can take much longer.

When you start to download a file, you might get a message telling you that you need to install a plug-in first. Go to the above section on plug-ins to figure out what you need to do.

When you are ready to download the file, follow the directions closely. Most of the sites mentioned in this book are very good about describing what you need to do. Before you begin, you may want to PRINT THE DIRECTIONS so you can read them even after you have closed your browser and rebooted your computer. Downloaded files are usually saved to a temporary directory on your hard drive by your online service or browser. Look for a folder called "temp" or "download."

In that folder you will see a file that usually says "setup.exe." Click on that file and the installation will begin. From here on out, breathe a sigh of relief. The process is usually very easy and self-explanatory. The file will show up as an icon on your desktop once the process is complete. Click on that icon and the electronic application will appear.

For more on downloading, go to wp.netscape.com/download.

What if I'm still having problems?

Ideally, you should ask someone in your family or neighborhood who is familiar with computers for help. Each computer has its own quirks— and trouble shooting is easiest when done by someone who knows the type of computer you are using.

If you are using an online service or ISP, call customer service. Sometimes you have to spend time on hold, but the staff should be able to help you. You may also find answers at an online help area, such as the AOL Computing Channel (keyword: computing) or CompuServe's Customer Service Help Database ("go" to "cshelp"). Otherwise, try your local library for general books devoted to using the Internet. They contain more advice than can be provided here, and they offer specific tips for your computer.

The Web, as well, provides help. Try the Netscape home page at www.netscape.com, the Microsoft home page at www.microsoft.com or your online service's Internet section.

Are there any good Internet sites for "newbies"?

Still confused? While bookstores are loaded with dictionaries and "how-to" books, not surprisingly, you can also find them on line, free.

**Newbies Anonymous: A Newcomer's
Guide to the Internet**
www.geocities.com/TheTropics/1945/index1.htm

Folks Online: For the World's Non-Technical Majority
www.folksonline.com

Internet Glossaries
www.netlingo.com
www.netdictionary.com

Netiquette
www.albion.com/netiquette

GOOD LUCK,
AND HAPPY SURFING!

INDICES

Appendix 3
An Index to Every Internet Address in this Book

Name	Address (URLs, etc.)	What's inside
Getting Plugged In		
The List	www.thelist.com	List of Internet Service Providers
Google Groups	groups.google.com	Access to newsgroups
Collecting Information About Colleges		
COOL's Web search	nces.ed.gov/ipeds/cool/Search.asp	Database of college descriptions
Peterson's College Search	www.petersons.com	Database of college descriptions
College Board Search	www.collegeboard.com	Database of college descriptions
Princeton Review's Counselor-O-Matic	www.princetonreview.com/college/research	Database of college descriptions
XAP's Mentor Web Sites	www.xap.com/gotocollege	Database of college descriptions
Best College Picks, from Peterson's	www.bestcollegepicks.com	Database of college descriptions
Colleges Want You, from Peterson's	www.collegeswantyou.com	Database of college descriptions w/ reverse search
CollegeNET Search	cnsearch.collegenet.com	Database of college descriptions
Find Your Ideal School, by U.S. News	www.usnews.com/usnews/edu/college/tools/brief/cosearch-brief.php	
CollegeXpress	www.collegexpress.com	Database of college descriptions
The College Guide	www.mycollegeguide.org	Database of college descriptions
CollegeView Search	www.collegeview.com/collegesearch/index.epl	Database of college descriptions
Looking for Specific Types of Schools		
HBCU Central	www.hbcu-central.com	Browsable information on historically black colleges
Hillel	www.hillel.org	Browsable information on Hillel at US Colleges
Jesuit Colleges	www.ajcunet.edu	Browsable information on Jesuit colleges

Name	Address (URLs, etc.)	What's inside
Studyabroad.com	www.studyabroad.com	Browsable information on study-abroad programs
Collegeabroad.com	www.collegeabroad.com	Browsable information on study-abroad programs
Finding and Using to College Home Pages		
FastSEARCH	www.fastWeb.monster.com/fastsearch/college	Links to home pages of colleges in the U.S.
YAHOO!'s College Listings—United States	dir.yahoo.com/Education/Higher_Education/ Colleges_and_Universities	Links to home pages of colleges in the U.S.
U.S. Universities and Community Colleges	www.utexas.edu/world/univ	Links to home pages of colleges in the U.S.
All About College	www.allaboutcollege.com	Links to home pages of colleges around the world
Independent Higher Education Network	www.fihe.org/tools/map.asp	Links to home pages of private colleges
Canadian Colleges	www.uwaterloo.ca/canu/index.html	Links to home pages of Canadian colleges
Women's College Coalition	www.womenscolleges.org	Links to home pages of women's colleges
Community College Web	www.mcli.dist.maricopa.edu/cc	Links to home pages of two-year colleges
Community College Finder	www.aacc.nche.edu	Links to home pages of two-year colleges
Professional and Graduate Schools	www.gradschools.com/search.html	Links to home pages of graduate schools
American Indian Higher Education Consortium	www.aihec.org	Links to home pages of tribal colleges
Hispanic Association of American Colleges	www.hacu.net	Links to home pages of Hispanic-Serving Institutions
Reading College Newspapers		
U-Wire	www.uwire.com	Links to top stories from student newspapers
College News Online	www.collegenews.com	Links to top stories from student newspapers
News Link	www.newslink.org/statcamp.html	Links to newspapers around the country
Chronicle of Higher Education	chronicle.com	News about higher education
Getting the Regional Scoop		
Houston Area Higher Education Resources	www.chron.com/content/community/higher_ed/index.html	Information about colleges in the Houston area
The New York Times' Education Coverage	www.nytimes.com/pages/education.html	Information about colleges in NY and elsewhere
Southern California Schools and Colleges	www.latimes.com/news/learning	Information about colleges in Southern California
The Washington CollegePost	washingtonpost.com/wp-dyn/education/highereducation	Information about colleges in Washington, DC
Thinking About Safety		
Security on Campus, Inc.	www.campussafety.org	Information about crime on campus

Name	Address (URLs, etc.)	What's inside
What About College Rankings?		
U.S. News & World Report	www.usnews.com/usnews/ edu/college/cohome.htm	College rankings
Princeton Review's 351 Best Colleges	www.princetonreview.com/college/research	Colleges ranked by students
Maclean's University Rankings	www.macleans.ca	Canadian college rankings
Laissaez-Faire Rankings	collegeadmissions.tripod.com	Colleges ranked by selectivity criteria
College Ranking Service	www.rankyourcollege.com	College rankings, tongue-in-cheek
College and University Rankings	www.library.uiuc.edu/edx/rankings.htm	Comprehensive site about college rankings
Evaluating Information Technology on Campus	www.educause.edu/consumerguide	Questions to ask about campus technology
Preparing for a Campus Tour		
College Board on College Visits	www.collegeboard.com/csearch/college_visits	Thinking about location
CitySearch	www.citysearch.com	Research your future hometown
DigitalCity	www.digitalcity.com	Research your future hometown
MapQuest	www.mapquest.com	Get directions to college campuses
Taking a Campus Tour—Virtually		
CampusTours.com	www.campustours.com	Index of virtual tours and Web cams
CollegeView's Virtual Tours	www.collegeview.com	Index of virtual tours
Collegiate Choice Walking Tours	www.collegiatechoice.com	Catalog of indepth videos of campus walking tours
Gathering More Advice		
Starting Points for Parents and Students	www.collegeboard.com	Guidance on college selection
About.Com's College-Admission Guide	collegeapps.about.com	Human guidance on admissions
U.S. News's College Forums	www.usnews.com/usnews/edu/forums.fohome.html	The most vexing questions
Bolt	www.bolt.com	Boards and chat groups
College Comparison Worksheet	www.usnews.com/usnews/edu/college/cohome.htm	Online worksheet
College Personality Quiz	www.usnews.com/usnews/edu/college/tools/cpq/coquiz.htm	Online worksheet
Dear Admissions Guru...	www.mycollegeguide.org/guru	Occasional articles on selecting a college
Getting Ready for University	www.campusaccess.com	Essay on how to choose the right college
Princeton Review's Forums	discuss.princetonreview.com	Online discussions about choosing a college
Soc.college.admissions	Soc.college.admissions	Q-and-A bulletin board
Soc.college	Soc.college	Q-and-A bulletin board

Name	Address (URLs, etc.)	What's inside
Do Some Interviews of Your Own		
World Alumni Net	www.Alumni.Net	Direct links to college alums
The Daily Jolt	www.dailyjolt.com	Links to student forums and home pages
Learning About Distance Education		
Council for Higher Education Accreditation	www.chea.org	Directory of accrediting agencies
Distance Education and Training Council	www.detc.org	Directory of accredited distance ed programs
World Wide Learn	www.worldwidelearn.com	Directory of online courses and programs
Peterson's Distance Learning	www.petersons.com/distancelearning	Directory of online courses and programs
Globewide Network Academy	www.gnacademy.org	Catalog of online courses
DANTES	www.dantes.doded.mil	Catalog of online courses
Virtual University Gazette	www.geteducated.com/vugaz.htm	Electronic newsletter on distance education
Degree.Net	www.degree.net	Background information on distance education
Yahoo's List of Distance Education Options	dir.yahoo.com/Education/Distance_Learning	List of distance education sites
Yahoo's Overview of Distance Education	degrees.education.yahoo.com	Overview of distance education opportunities
alt.education.distance	alt.education.distance	Distance education newsgroup
A Sampling of Distance-Ed Programs		
Capella University	www.capellauniversity.edu	Accredited online university
CIC Course Share	www.cic.uiuc.edu	Online education at Big 10 Schools
iLearning at Parkland College	online.parkland.edu	Links to online course providers, and courses
Jones International University	www.jonesinternational.edu	Accredited Online university
New School Online University	www.dialnsa.edu	Online undergrad degree offered by New School
Servicemembers Opportunity College	www.soc.aascu.org	Online degrees for servicemembers and their families
Southern Regional Electronic Campus	www.electroniccampus.org	Online education at southern universities
SUNY Learning Network	sln.suny.edu	Online education at State University of NY schools
University of Phoenix	www.phoenix.edu	Online business education
Western Governors University	www.wgu.edu	Virtual university
Cooperative Education		
National Commission for Cooperative Education	www.co-op.edu	Online guide to co-op
Cooperative Education Association	www.ceainc.org	Links to co-op sites
Cooperative Education Network	www.ocasppcp.uc.edu/home	Links to co-op sites
Co-op Student Handbook	www.coope.neu.edu	Online guide to co-op

Name	Address (URLs, etc.)	What's inside
Antioch College's Co-op Ed Survival Guide	www.antioch-college.edu/co_op	List of co-op opportunities
Studentjobs.gov	www.studentjobs.gov/d_coop.asp	Cooperative Education with the Federal Government
Those Stressful Standardized Tests		
College Admissions Tests and Related Aid	icpac.indiana.edu/publications/infoseries/is-11.xml	Standardized testing information
SAT Dates	www.collegeboard.com/student/testing/sat/calenfees.html	Standardized testing information
Online SAT Registration	www.collegeboard.com/testing	Standardized testing information
Educational Testing Service Network	www.ets.org	Standardized testing information
ACT's Web site	www.actstudent.org	Standardized testing information
ACT Assessment Test Dates	www.actstudent.org/regist/currentdates.html	Standardized testing information
Registering for the ACT Assessment	www.actstudent.org/regist	Standardized testing information
Wordsmyth S.A.T. Dictionary	www.lightlink.com/bobp/wedt/sat.htm	Dictionary of words that appear on SAT
TestU	www.testu.com	Free, online prep
Peterson's Test Prep	www.petersons.com/testprepchannel	Online test prep
Kaplan's Test Prep	www.kaptest.com	Online test prep
Princeton Review	www.princetonreview.com/college/testPrep	Online test prep
College Power Prep	www.powerprep.com	Online test prep
Study Hall	www.studyhall.com	Online test prep
College Board's SAT Prep Center	apps.collegeboard.com/satprep/index.jsp	Online test prep
Apex Learning—Online Courses for AP Exams	www.apexlearning.com	Online AP courses
AP Help from the College Board	www.collegeboard.com/student/testing/ap/about.html	Info about AP tests
New SAT	www.collegeboard.com/student/testing/newsat/about.html	Preview of the New SAT
Online Applications		
Apply Online	www.princetonreview.com/college/apply	Online applications
CollegeNET's ApplyWeb Online Applications	www.applyweb.com	Online applications
XAP Applications	www.xap.com/apply	Online applications
Next Stop College	www.collegeboard.com/apply	Online applications
The Common Application	app.commonapp.org	Direct link to the electronic Common Application
Ugh! The Essay		
Writing the College Admission Essay	icpac.indiana.edu/publications/infoseries/is-15.html	Advice on writing college essays
IvyEssays	www.ivyessays.com	Free advice and fee-based essay services
EssayEdge	www.essayedge.com	Free advice and fee-based essay services
Cambridge Essay Service	www.world.std.com/~edit	Free advice and fee-based essay services

Name	Address (URLs, etc.)	What's inside
Useful References For Any Writer		
Wordsmyth Educational Dictionary-Thesaurus	www.wordsmyth.net	Online dictionary
Thesaurus	www.thesaurus.com	Online version of Roget's Thesaurus
Dictionary	www.dictionary.com	Online dictionary
The Slot	www.theslot.com	Online style manual
The Elements of Style	www.bartleby.com	The classic guide to effective writing
Don't Forget the Interview		
Princeton Review's interview advice	www.princetonreview.com/college	Interview advice
Your Virtual Interview	www.bergen.org/AAST/Projects/CollegePrep/Interview.html	Virtual Interview Practice
College Admissions Office E-mail Addresses	www.college-scholarships.com	Links to admission offices' E-mail addresses
Dealing with Recommendations		
Secondary School Report Form	www.nacac.com/downloads.html	For guidance counselors
National Association for College Adm. Counseling	www.nacac.com	For guidance counselors
Financial Aid—Thinking Ahead		
Kiplinger's Personal Finance Magazine	www.kiplinger.com	Investing for college
Money Magazine	www.money.cnn.com/pf/101/lessons/11	Investing for college
SmartMoney Magazine	www.smartmoney.com/college	Investing for college
Financial Aid Calculators	www.finaid.org/calculators	Fifteen calculators designed for college planning The
College Board's Financial Aid Services	www.collegeboard.com/pay	Information about saving for college
Fidelity	www.fidelity.com	Investment advice
Morningstar	www.morningstar.com	Investment advice
Vanguard	www.vanguard.com	Investment advice
The Street	www.thestreet.com	Investment advice
Quicken	www.quicken.com	Investment advice
The Motley Fool	www.fool.com	Investment advice
Financial Aid 101		
FinAid! The Smart Student's Guide to Financial Aid	www.finaid.org	Information on loans, scholarships, and scams
Students.Gov	www.students.gov	Department of Education's central student aid site
College is Possible	www.collegeispossible.org	About college planning
FastWeb's Parents Page	www.fastweb.monster.com/fastweb/content/parents/index.ptml	About paying for college

Name	Address (URLs, etc.)	What's inside
Wired Scholar	www.wiredscholar.com	About loans
Mapping Your Future	www.mapping-your-future.org/paying	About paying for college
California Student Aid Commission	www.csac.ca.gov	About paying for college
California Student Aid Commission	www.edfund.org	About paying for college
Illinois Student Assistance Commission	www.collegezone.org	About paying for college
Texas Guaranteed Student Loan Corporation	www.tgslc.org	About paying for college
Texas Guaranteed Student Loan Corporation	www.AdventuresinEducation.org	About paying for college
Soc.college.financial-aid	Soc.college.financial-aid	Advice and commiseration
Applying for Financial Aid		
Expected Family Contribution calculator	www.collegeboard.com/pay	Calculator for figuring out your EFC
FAFSA on the Web	www.fafsa.ed.gov	Web-based version of the FAFSA
Personal Identification Number	www.pin.ed.gov	Apply for a personal identification number
PROFILE	profileonline.collegeboard.com	PROFILE Registration and Q-and-A
Federal Student Aid		
The Student Guide	www.studentaid.ed.gov/guide	The government's guide to federal student aid
Office of Postsecondary Education	www.ed.gov/about/offices/list/OPE/index.html	Technical resources from the Dept. of Education
Federal Student Loans		
Direct Loan Program	www.ed.gov/DirectLoan	Government information on direct lending
eStudentLoan	www.estudentloan.com	Compare lenders
Sallie Mae	www.salliemae.com	Information on loans and the company itself
Banks, Guaranty Agencies, and More		
Yahoo's List of Lenders	dir.yahoo.com/Education/Financial_Aid/Loans	Links to sites maintained by lenders
Access Group	www.accessgroup.org	Source for federal student loans
ASAP/Union Bank and Trust	www.asapubt.com	Source for federal student loans
Bank of America	www.bankofamerica.com/studentbanking	Source for federal student loans
BankOne	www.educationone.com	Source for federal student loans
Chase Manhattan	www.chase.com/educationfirst	Source for federal student loans
Chela Financial Services	www.loans4students.org	Source for federal student loans
Citibank	www.studentloan.com	Source for federal student loans

Name	Address (URLs, etc.)	What's inside
Educaid	www.educaid.com	Source for federal student loans
Fleet	www.fleet.com/education	Source for federal student loans
Key Education Resources	www.key.com/education	Source for federal student loans
LoanStar Student Program	www.loanstar.com	Source for federal student loans
National City	www.nationalcity.com	Source for federal student loans
PNC Bank	www.eduloans.pncbank.com	Source for federal student loans
Southwest Student Services	www.sssc.com	Source for federal student loans
Student Loan Funding	www.studentloanfunding.org	Source for federal student loans
SunTrust Bank	www.suntrusteducation.com	Source for federal student loans
US Bank	www.usbank.com/studentloans	Source for federal student loans
Wells Fargo	wellsfargo.com/per/accounts/student	Source for federal student loans
LoanLocator	www.nslc.org	Track your student loans
State Guaranty Agencies	bcol02.ed.gov/Programs/EROD/org_list.cfm	List of state loan guaranty agencies

Tax Cuts Explained

HOPE Scholarship and Lifetime Learning Credits	www.ed.gov/offices/OPE/PPI/HOPE	Guide to Hope Scholarships and more
Ec. Growth & Tax Relief Reconciliation Act of 2001	www.house.gov/rules/1836_sum.pdf	Summary of 2001 tax changes
The Motley Fool	www.fool.com/taxes/taxcenter	Information about education IRAs, tax planning
IRS Tax Benefits for Education	www.irs.gov/individuals/students/index.html	Information about education tax benefits from the IRS
IRS Tax Benefits for Education	www.irs.gov/pub/irs-pdf/p970.pdf	Information about education tax benefits from the IRS

State-Based Student Aid

State Education Agencies	bcol02.ed.gov/Programs/EROD/org_list.cfm	Links to state-specific sites on financial aid
State Higher-Education Agencies	bcol02.ed.gov/Programs/EROD/org_list.cfm	Links to state-specific sites on financial aid
College Savings Plans Network	www.collegesavings.org	Directory of state-based college savings plans
Internet Guide to "529" Plans	www.savingforcollege.com	Comparison of state-based college savings plans

Collegiate-Based Student Aid

Financial Aid Office Web Pages	www.finaid.org/otheraid/fao.phtml	Links to colleges' financial-aid offices
College Aid Offices	www.yahoo.com/Education/Financial_Aid	Links to colleges' financial-aid offices

Name	Address (URLs, etc.)	What's inside
Focusing on Scholarships		
FastWeb	www.fastWeb.monster.com	Personalized scholarship-search service
MACH25	www.collegenet.com/mach25	Personalized scholarship-search service
ExPAN Scholarship Search	www.collegeboard.org/pay	Scholarship-search service
WiredScholar (from Sallie Mae)	www.wiredscholar.com	Database of scholarship programs
Pacific NW Scholarship Guide	www.collegeplan.org/cpnow/pnwguide/pnwguide.htm	Scholarship-search service for Pacific NW students
Scholarship Research Network	www.smexpress.com	Scholarship-search service
United Negro College Fund	www.uncf.org	Scholarships typically for minority students
Gates Millenium Scholarship Program	www.gmsp.org	Scholarship fund for low-income minority students
Black Excel	www.blackexcel.org	Browse scholarship services for minority students
American Society of Association Executives	www.asaenet.org	Links to 1700 associations on the Web
Foundation Center	www.fdncenter.org/funders	Links to private foundations
Don't Get Scammed		
Scholarship Scams	www.ftc.gov/bcp/conline/edcams/scholarship	Tips on spotting scams
Evaluating Scholarship Matching Services	www.finaid.org/scholarships/matching.phtml	Protecting yourself from scams
Considering the Military		
Military.com	www.military.com/Careers/Education	Information on military programs and careers
ROTC Headquarters	www.defenselink.mil/faq/pis/19.html	Information on ROTC
GI Bill Web Site	www.gibill.va.gov	Information on the GI Bill
My (Military) Future	www.myfuture.com	Information on ROTC and other military programs
Considering Community Service		
Americorps	www.americorps.gov	Information on AmeriCorps
Corporation for National Service	www.nationalservice.org	Information on National Service
Presidential Freedom Scholars	www.nationalservice.org/scholarships	Information on Presidential Freedom Awards
CityYear	www.cityyear.org	Information on City-Year's service programs
For Future Health Professionals		
National Health Service Corps	nhsc.bhpr.hrsa.gov	Federal money for soon-to-be nurses and doctors
Bureau of Health Professions	bhpr.hrsa.gov/nursing/aid.htm	Federal money for soon-to-be nurses and doctors

Name	Address (URLs, etc.)	What's inside
If You're an Athlete		
NCAA Guide for College-Bound Student-Athletes	www.ncaa.org/eligibility/cbsa	NCAA guide to scholarships, recruiting, and eligibility
NJCAA Guide for Athletes	www.njcaa.org	Sports programs at Junior Colleges
Women's Sports Foundation	www.womenssportsfoundation.org	Sports information for women
Student MVP	studentmvp.com	Recruiting service
CollegeRecruiting	collegerecruiting.com	Recruiting service
Scout USA	www.scoutusa.com	Recruiting service
Prepstar	prepstar.com	Recruiting service
College Prospects of America	www.cpoa.com	Recruiting service
College Bound Student Alliance	www.collegepartnership.com/athletics.html	Recruiting service
National Directory of College Athletics	www.collegiatedirectories.com	E-mail addresses for college coaches
Commercial Education Loans		
eStudent Loan	www.estudentloan.com	Side by side comparison of private loans
The Education Research Institute	www.teri.org	Source for private loans
Nellie Mae	www.nelliemae.com	Source for private loans
PLATO	www.plato.org	Source for private loans
GATE	www.gateloan.com	Source for private loans
International Education Finance Corporation	www.IEFC.com	Source for private loans for study abroad
Installment Plans		
TuitionPay from Academic Management Service	www.tuitionpay.com	Administers monthly-payment plans
Tuition Management Systems	www.afford.com	Administers monthly-payment plans
A Few More Radical Options		
ECollegeBid	www.ecollegebid.com	Bid on college tuition
Sage Tuition Rewards Program	www.student-aid.com	Investment program for parents
UPromise	www.upromise.com	Investment program for parents
BabyMint	www.babymint.com	Investment program for parents
My Rich Uncle	www.myrichuncle.com	Loan alternative
Second Chances		
Annual Student Vacancy Survey	www.nebhe.org/vacancy_survey.html	Survey of colleges in New England with openings
NACAC Space Availability Survey	www.nacac.com/survey/results.cfm	Survey of NACAC colleges with openings

Name	Address (URLs, etc.)	What's inside
Cyber-College Life (in ABC order)		
#1 Free Stuff	www.1freestuff.com	Free stuff on the web
Black Collegian Online	www.black-collegian.com	Articles, chat rooms, and links to college life sites
Campus Access	www.campusaccess.com	Articles, essays
College Club	www.collegeclub.com	Articles, chat rooms, and links to college life sites
College Television Network	www.mtvu.com	Segments on college life
Colleges.com	www.colleges.com	Articles, chat and tools
CampusEStore.com	www.campusestore.com	Discounts for students
GreekPages	www.greekpages.com	Articles and links to sites about greek life
GreekSource	www.greeksource.com	Articles, links on fraternity and sorority life
Internet Guide to Spring Break	www.springbreak.com	Links to information on spring break
Pick-a-Prof	www.pick-a-prof.com	Faculty evaluations
Roomate Service.com	www.roommates.com	Roommate matching service
StudentAdvantage.Com	www.studentadvantage.com	Discounts, articles, tools
Student.Com	www.student.com	Articles, chat rooms, and links to college life sites
Student Counseling Virtual Pamphlet Collection	counseling.uchicago.edu/vpc/virtulets.html	Links to virtual pamphlets on counseling topics
Universal Black Pages	www.ubp.com	Articles and links to sites about HBCUs
Google's list of e-zines	directory.google.com/Top/News/Colleges_and_Universities/ Magazines_and_E-zines	Links to more college-life magazines
Yahoo!'s list of e-zines	dir.yahoo.com/News_and_Media/College_and_University/ Magazines	Links to more college-life magazines
E-Campus Bookstores and Online Class Notes		
Best Book Buys	www.bestbookbuys.com	Searches online bookstores for best buys
EFollett	www.Efollet.com	Online source for college textbooks
Varsity Books	www.varsitybooks.com	Online source for college textbooks
Big Words	www.bigwords.com	Online source for college textbooks
E Campus	www.ecampus.com	Online source for college textbooks
ClassBook	www.classbook.com	Online source for used college textbooks
The DORM Store	www.dormtours.net/eshop.asp	An online shop tailored for college-bound students
MIT OpenCourseWare	web.mit.edu/ocw	Online class notes for MIT
YourNotes	www.yournotes.com	Online class notes for UPenn
Plagiarism.org	www.plagiarism.org	Site to help professors catch online plagiarists
Turn It In	www.turnitin.com	Site to help professors catch online plagiarists
IEssay Verification Engine (EVE)	www.canexus.com/eve	Site to help professors catch online plagiarists

Name	Address (URLs, etc.)	What's inside
Metasites (in ABC order)		
@theU	www.attheu.com	UniBucks, career center, searches, shopping, and more
About.Com's College Admission page	collegeapps.about.com	Human guidance, links, Q-and-A
America Online's College Planning Areas	Keyword: College	Searches, links, chats, Financial planning, more
Black Excel	www.blackexcel.org	Financial aid, advice for black college-bound student
College Board Online	www.collegeboard.com	Searches, Q-and-A areas, and more
College Guide	www.mycollegeguide.org	Searches, Articles, and more
CollegeNET	www.collegenet.com	Searches, Q-and-A areas, and more
College Planning	www.collegeplan.org	Searches, Advice, and more
College Prep 101	collegeprep.okstate.edu	Searches, Articles, and more
CollegeView	www.collegeview.com	Searches, Q-and-A areas, and more
CollegeXpress	www.collegexpress.com	Searches, Q-and-A areas, and more
EduPrep	www.eduprep.com	Searches, Articles, Test Prep and more
FinAid Page	www.finaid.org	Financial-aid guides, Q-and-A areas, and more Go
College	www.gocollege.com	Scholarship news, and more
Guidance On Line	home.cfl.rr.com/nwunder/guidance.html	Advice, links, and more
MyRoad.com	www.myroad.com	Searches, Career Information, and more
Peterson's Education Portal	www.petersons.com	Searches, Q-and-A areas, and more
Princeton Review	www.princetonreview.com	Searches, Articles, Test Prep and more
ScholarStuff	www.scholarstuff.com	Searches, Q-and-A areas, and more
WiredScholar	www.wiredscholar.com	Searches, Q-and-A areas, and more
Getting Ready for Graduate School		
Student Doctor Network	www.studentdoctor.net	Searches, Articles, Advice and more for Pre-meds
Find Law	stu.findlaw.com/prelaw	Searches, Articles, Advice and more for Pre-laws
Internet Legal Resource Guide	www.ilrg.com/pre-law.html	Searches, Articles, Advice and more for Pre-laws
Law Students	www.law.com/jsp/students.jsp	Searches, Articles, Advice and more for Pre-laws
MBA Pathfinder	www.mba.com	Searches, Articles, Advice and more for Pre-bness

Name	Address (URLs, etc.)	What's inside
Free E-Mail Services		
Big Foot	www.bigfoot.com	Commercial e-mail provider
CollegeClub	www.collegeclub.com	Commercial e-mail provider
Hotmail	www.hotmail.com	Commercial e-mail provider
Lycos	comm.lycos.com	Commercial e-mail provider
Mail.com	www.mail.com	Commercial e-mail provider
Mail2Web	www.mail2web.com	Check e-mail while away from your computer
E-Mail Privacy Services		
ZixMail	www.zixmail.com	privacy enhancements to existing email
ZipLip.com	www.ziplip.com	private e-mail accounts
HushMail.com	www.hushmail.com	private e-mail accounts
Internet Search Services		
Google Groups	groups.google.com	Search engine for Usenet newsgroups
Google	www.google.com	Search engine and catalog of the Web
Google Toolbar	toolbar.google.com	Google toolbar for your desktop
Yahoo!	www.yahoo.com	Search engine and catalog of the Web
Alltheweb	www.alltheweb.com	Search engine and catalog of the Web
Teoma	www.teoma.com	Search engine and catalog of the Web
AltaVista	www.altavista.com	Search engine and catalog of the Web
AOL Search	Keyword: search	AOL directory and Web search engine
MSN Search	search.msn.com	Search engine and directory
Lycos	www.lycos.com	Search engine and catalog of the Web
Netscape Search	search.netscape.com	"Open Directory" plus search engine
Metasearch Engines		
Dogpile	www.dogpile.com	Metasearch engine
Mamma.com	www.mamma.com	Metasearch engine
Search	www.search.com	Metasearch engine
Metacrawler	www.metacrawler.com	Metasearch engine

Name	Address (URLs, etc.)	What's inside
Online Help		
Information on downloading	wp.netscape.com/download	Online help
AOL Computing Channel	Keyword: computing	Online help
CompuServe's Customer Service	"go" to "cshelp"	Online help
Netscape's home page	www.netscape.com	Online help
Microsoft's home page	www.microsoft.com	Online help
Internet Sites for Newbies		
Newbies Anonymous: A Guideto the Internet	www.geocities.com/TheTropics/1945/index1.htm	An Internet introduction
Folks Online: For the World's Non-Technical Majority	www.folksonline.com	An Internet introduction
NetLingo	www.netlingo.com	An Internet glossary
NetDictionary	www.netdictionary.com	An Internet glossary
Netiquette	www.albion.com/netiquette	An introduction to netiquette

Alphabetical Index of Web Sites

Name	Address (URLs, etc.)	What's inside
#1 Free Stuff	www.1freestuff.com	Free stuff on the web
@theU	www.attheu.com	UniBucks, career center, searches, shopping, and more
About.Com's College-Admission Guide	collegeapps.about.com	Human guidance on admissions
Access Group	www.accessgroup.org	Source for federal student loans
ACT Registration	www.actstudent.org/regist	Standardized testing information
ACT Test Dates	www.actstudent.org/regist/currentdates.html	Standardized testing information
ACT Web Site	www.actstudent.org	Standardized testing information
All About College	www.allaboutcollege.com	Links to home pages of colleges around the world
Alltheweb	www.alltheweb.com	Search engine and catalog of the Web
alt.education.distance	alt.education.distance	Distance education newsgroup
AltaVista	www.altavista.com	Search engine and catalog of the Web
American Indian Higher Education Consortium	www.aihec.org	Links to home pages of tribal colleges
American Society of Association Executives	www.asaenet.org	Links to 1700 associations on the Web
Americorps	www.americorps.gov	Information on AmeriCorps
Annual Student Vacancy Survey	www.nebhe.org/vacancy_survey.html	Survey of colleges in New England with openings
Antioch College's Co-op Ed Survival Guide	www.antioch-college.edu/co_op	List of co-op opportunities
AOL College Planning Areas	Keyword: College	Searches, links, chats, Financial planning, more
AOL Computing Channel	Keyword: computing	Online help
AOL Search	Keyword: search	AOL directory and Web search engine
AP Help from the College Board	www.collegeboard.com/student/testing/ap/about.html	Info about AP tests
Apex Learning-Online Courses for AP Exams	www.apexlearning.com	Online AP courses
Apply Online	www.princetonreview.com/college/apply	Online applications
ASAP/Union Bank and Trust	www.asapubt.com	Source for federal student loans
BabyMint	www.babymint.com	Investment program for parents
Bank of America	www.bankofamerica.com/studentbanking	Source for federal student loans
BankOne	www.educationone.com	Source for federal student loans
Best Book Buys	www.bestbookbuys.com	Searches online bookstores for best buys
Best College Picks, from Peterson's	www.bestcollegepicks.com	Database of college descriptions

Name	Address (URLs, etc.)	What's inside
Big Foot	www.bigfoot.com	Commercial e-mail provider
Big Words	www.bigwords.com	Online source for college textbooks
Black Collegian Online	www.black-collegian.com	Articles, chat rooms, and links to college life sites
Black Excel	www.blackexcel.org	Financial aid, advice for black college-bound student
Bolt	www.bolt.com	Boards and chat groups
Bureau of Health Professions	bhpr.hrsa.gov/nursing/aid.htm	Federal money for soon-to-be nurses and doctors
California Student Aid Commission	www.csac.ca.gov	About paying for college
California Student Aid Commission	www.edfund.org	About paying for college
Cambridge Essay Service	www.world.std.com/~edit	Free advice and fee-based essay services
Campus Access	www.campusaccess.com	Articles, essays
CampusEstore.com	www.campusestore.com	Discounts for students
CampusTours.com	www.campustours.com	Index of virtual tours and Web cams
Canadian Colleges	www.uwaterloo.ca/canu/index.html	Links to home pages of Canadian colleges
Capella University	www.capellauniversity.edu	Accredited online university
Chase Manhattan	www.chase.com/educationfirst	Source for federal student loans
Chela Financial Services	www.loans4students.org	Source for federal student loans
Chronicle of Higher Education	chronicle.com	News about higher education
CIC Course Share	www.cic.uiuc.edu	Online education at Big 10 Schools
Citibank	www.studentloan.com	Source for federal student loans
CitySearch	www.citysearch.com	Research your future hometown
CityYear	www.cityyear.org	Information on City-Year's service programs
ClassBook	www.classbook.com	Online source for used college textbooks
College Admissions Office E-mail Addresses	www.college-scholarships.com	Links to admission offices' E-mail addresses
College Admissions Tests and Related Aid	icpac.indiana.edu/publications/infoseries/is-11.xml	Standardized testing information
College Aid Offices	www.yahoo.com/Education/Financial_Aid	Links to colleges' financial-aid offices
College and University Rankings	www.library.uiuc.edu/edx/rankings.htm	Comprehensive site about college rankings
College Board on College Visits	www.collegeboard.com/csearch/college_visits	Thinking about location
College Board Online	www.collegeboard.com	Searches, Q-and-A areas, and more
College Board's Financial Aid Services	www.collegeboard.com/pay	Information about saving for college
College Board's SAT Prep Center	apps.collegeboard.com/satprep/index.jsp	Online test prep
College Bound Student Alliance	www.collegepartnership.com/athletics.html	Recruiting service
College Club	www.collegeclub.com	Articles, chat rooms, and links to college life sites
College Comparison Worksheet	www.usnews.com/usnews/edu/college/cohome.htm	Online worksheet
College Guide	www.mycollegeguide.org	Searches, Articles, and more

Name	Address (URLs, etc.)	What's inside
College is Possible	www.collegeispossible.org	About college planning
College News Online	www.collegenews.com	Links to top stories from student newspapers
College Personality Quiz	www.usnews.com/usnews/edu/college/tools/cpq/coquiz.htm	Online worksheet
College Planning	www.collegeplan.org	Searches, Advice, and more
College Power Prep	www.powerprep.com	Online test prep
College Prep 101	collegeprep.okstate.edu	Searches, Articles, and more
College Prospects of America	www.cpoa.com	Recruiting service
College Ranking Service	www.rankyourcollege.com	College rankings, tongue-in-cheek
College Savings Plans Network	www.collegesavings.org	Directory of state-based college savings plans
College Television Network	www.mtvu.com	Segments on college life
Collegeabroad.com	www.collegeabroad.com	Browsable information on study-abroad programs
CollegeNET	www.collegenet.com	Searches, Q-and-A areas, and more
CollegeNET's ApplyWeb Online Applications	www.applyweb.com	Online applications
CollegeRecruiting	collegerecruiting.com	Recruiting service
Colleges Want You, from Peterson's	www.collegeswantyou.com	Database of college descriptions w/ reverse search
Colleges.com	www.colleges.com	Articles, chat and tools
CollegeView	www.collegeview.com	Searches, Q-and-A areas, and more
CollegeView's Virtual Tours	www.collegeview.com	Index of virtual tours
CollegeXpress	www.collegexpress.com	Searches, Q-and-A areas, and more
Collegiate Choice Walking Tours	www.collegiatechoice.com	Catalog of indepth videos of campus walking tours
Common Application	app.commonapp.org	Direct link to the electronic Common Application
Community College Finder	www.aacc.nche.edu	Links to home pages of two-year colleges
Community College Web	www.mcli.dist.maricopa.edu/cc	Links to home pages of two-year colleges
CompuServe's Customer Service	"go to ""cshelp"""	Online help
COOL's Web search	nces.ed.gov/ipeds/cool/Search.asp	Database of college descriptions
Co-op Student Handbook	www.coope.neu.edu	Online guide to co-op
Cooperative Education Association	www.ceiainc.org	Links to co-op sites
Cooperative Education Network	www.ocasppcp.uc.edu/home	Links to co-op sites
Corporation for National Service	www.nationalservice.org	Information on National Service
Council for Higher Education Accreditation	www.chea.org	Directory of accrediting agencies
Daily Jolt	www.dailyjolt.com	Links to student forums and home pages
DANTES	www.dantes.doded.mil	Catalog of online courses
Dear Admissions Guru...	www.mycollegeguide.org/guru	Occasional articles on selecting a college
Degree.Net	www.degree.net	Background information on distance education

Name	Address (URLs, etc.)	What's inside
Dictionary	www.dictionary.com	Online dictionary
DigitalCity	www.digitalcity.com	Research your future hometown
Direct Loan Program	www.ed.gov/DirectLoan	Government information on direct lending
Distance Education and Training Council	www.detc.org	Directory of accredited distance ed programs
Dogpile	www.dogpile.com	Metasearch engine
DORM Store	www.dormtours.net/eshop.asp	An online shop tailored for college-bound students
E Campus	www.ecampus.com	Online source for college textbooks
Ec. Growth & Tax Relief Reconciliation Act of 2001	www.house.gov/rules/1836_sum.pdf	Summary of 2001 tax changes
ECollegeBid	www.ecollegebid.com	Bid on college tuition
Educaid	www.educaid.com	Source for federal student loans
Educational Testing Service Network	www.ets.org	Standardized testing information
EduPrep	www.eduprep.com	Searches, Articles, Test Prep and more
EFollett	www.Efollet.com	Online source for college textbooks
Elements of Style	www.bartleby.com	The classic guide to effective writing
Essay Verification Engine (EVE)	www.canexus.com/eve	Site to help professors catch online plagiarists
EssayEdge	www.essayedge.com	Free advice and fee-based essay services
eStudent Loan	www.estudentloan.com	Side by side comparison of private loans
Evaluating Information Technology on Campus	www.educause.edu/consumerguide	Questions to ask about campus technology
Evaluating Scholarship Matching Services	www.finaid.org/scholarships/matching.phtml	Protecting yourself from scams
ExPAN Scholarship Search	www.collegeboard.org/pay	Scholarship-search service
Expected Family Contribution calculator	www.collegeboard.com/pay	Calculator for figuring out your EFC
FAFSA on the Web	www.fafsa.ed.gov	Web-based version of the FAFSA
FastSEARCH	www.fastWeb.monster.com/fastsearch/college	Links to home pages of colleges in the U.S.
FastWeb	www.fastWeb.monster.com	Personalized scholarship-search service
Fidelity	www.fidelity.com	Investment advice
FinAid! The Smart Student's Guide to Financial Aid	www.finaid.org	Information on loans, scholarships, and scams
Financial Aid Calculators	www.finaid.org/calculators	Fifteen calculators designed for college planning
Financial Aid Office Web Pages	www.finaid.org/otheraid/fao.phtml	Links to colleges' financial-aid offices
Find Law	stu.findlaw.com/prelaw	Searches, Articles, Advice and more for Pre-laws
Fleet	www.fleet.com/education	Source for federal student loans
Folks Online: For the World's Non-Technical Majority	www.folksonline.com	An Internet introduction
Foundation Center	www.fdncenter.org/funders	Links to private foundations

Name	Address (URLs, etc.)	What's inside
GATE	www.gateloan.com	Source for private loans
Gates Millenium Scholarship Program	www.gmsp.org	Scholarship fund for low-income minority students
Getting Ready for University	www.campusaccess.com	Essay on how to choose the right college
GI Bill Web Site	www.gibill.va.gov	Information on the GI Bill
Globewide Network Academy	www.gnacademy.org	Catalog of online courses
Go College	www.gocollege.com	Scholarship news, and more
Google	www.google.com	Search engine and catalog of the Web
Google Groups	groups.google.com	Search engine for Usenet newsgroups
Google Toolbar	toolbar.google.com	Google toolbar for your desktop
Google's list of e-zines	directory.google.com/Top/News/Colleges_and_Universities/Magazines_and_E-zines	
GreekPages	www.greekpages.com	Links to more college-life magazines
GreekSource	www.greeksource.com	Articles and links to sites about greek life
Guidance On Line	home.cfl.rr.com/nwunder/guidance.html	Articles, links on fraternity and sorority life
		Advice, links, and more
HBCU Central	www.hbcu-central.com	Browsable information on historically black colleges
Hillel	www.hillel.org	Browsable information on Hillel at US Colleges
Hispanic Association of American Colleges	www.hacu.net	Links to home pages of Hispanic-Serving Institutions
HOPE Scholarship and Lifetime Learning Credits	www.ed.gov/offices/OPE/PPI/HOPE	Guide to Hope Scholarships and more
Hotmail	www.hotmail.com	Commercial e-mail provider
Houston Area Higher Education Resources	www.chron.com/content/community/higher_ed/index.html	Information about colleges in the Houston area
HushMail.com	www.hushmail.com	private e-mail accounts
iLearning at Parkland College	online.parkland.edu	Links to online course providers, and courses
Illinois Student Assistance Commission	www.collegezone.org	About paying for college
Independent Higher Education Network	www.fihe.org/tools/map.asp	Links to home pages of private colleges
Information on downloading	wp.netscape.com/download	Online help
International Education Finance Corporation	www.IEFC.com	Source for private loans for study abroad
Internet Guide to "529" Plans	www.savingforcollege.com	Comparison of state-based college savings plans
Internet Guide to Spring Break	www.springbreak.com	Links to information on spring break
Internet Legal Resource Guide	www.ilrg.com/pre-law.html	Searches, Articles, Advice and more for Pre-laws
IRS Tax Benefits for Education	www.irs.gov/individuals/students/index.html	Information about education tax benefits from the IRS
IRS Tax Benefits for Education	www.irs.gov/pub/irs-pdf/p970.pdf	Information about education tax benefits from the IRS
IvyEssays	www.ivyessays.com	Free advice and fee-based essay services

Name	Address (URLs, etc.)	What's inside
Jesuit Colleges	www.ajcunet.edu	Browsable information on Jesuit colleges
Jones International University	www.jonesinternational.edu	Accredited Online university
Kaplan's Test Prep	www.kaptest.com	Online test prep
Key Education Resources	www.key.com/education	Source for federal student loans
Kiplinger's Personal Finance Magazine	www.kiplinger.com	Investing for college
Laissaez-Faire Rankings	collegeadmissions.tripod.com	Colleges ranked by selectivity criteria
Law Students	www.law.com/jsp/students.jsp	Searches, Articles, Advice and more for Pre-laws
LoanLocator	www.nslc.org	Track your student loans
LoanStar Student Program	www.loanstar.com	Source for federal student loans
Lycos	comm.lycos.com	Commercial e-mail provider
Lycos	www.lycos.com	Search engine and catalog of the Web
MACH25	www.collegenet.com/mach25	Personalized scholarship-search service
Maclean's University Rankings	www.macleans.ca	Canadian college rankings
Mail.com	www.mail.com	Commercial e-mail provider
Mail2Web	www.mail2web.com	Check e-mail while away from your computer
Mamma.com	www.mamma.com	Metasearch engine
Mapping Your Future	www.mapping-your-future.org/paying	About paying for college
MapQuest	www.mapquest.com	Get directions to college campuses
MBA Pathfinder	www.mba.com	Searches, Articles, Advice and more for Pre-bness
Metacrawler	www.metacrawler.com	Metasearch engine
Microsoft's home page	www.microsoft.com	Online help
Military.com	www.military.com/Careers/Education	Information on military programs and careers
MIT OpenCourseWare	web.mit.edu/ocw	Online class notes for MIT
Money Magazine	www.money.cnn.com/pf/101/lessons/11	Investing for college
Morningstar	www.morningstar.com	Investment advice
Motley Fool	www.fool.com	Investment advice
Motley Fool	www.fool.com/taxes/taxcenter	Information about education IRAs, tax planning
MSN Search	search.msn.com	Search engine and directory
My (Military) Future	www.myfuture.com	Information on ROTC and other military programs
My Rich Uncle	www.myrichuncle.com	Loan alternative
MyRoad.com	www.myroad.com	Searches, Career Information, and more

Name	Address (URLs, etc.)	What's inside
NACAC Space Availability Survey	www.nacac.com/survey/results.cfm	Survey of NACAC colleges with openings
National Association for College Adm. Counseling	www.nacac.com	For guidance counselors
National City	www.nationalcity.com	Source for federal student loans
National Commission for Cooperative Education	www.co-op.edu	Online guide to co-op
National Directory of College Athletics	www.collegiatedirectories.com	E-mail addresses for college coaches
National Health Service Corps	nhsc.bhpr.hrsa.gov	Federal money for soon-to-be nurses and doctors
NCAA Guide for College-Bound Student-Athletes	www.ncaa.org/eligibility/cbsa	NCAA guide to scholarships, recruiting, and eligibility
Nellie Mae	www.nelliemae.com	Source for private loans
NetDictionary	www.netdictionary.com	An Internet glossary
Netiquette	www.albion.com/netiquette	An introduction to netiquette
NetLingo	www.netlingo.com	An Internet glossary
Netscape Search	search.netscape.com	Open Directory plus search engine
Netscape's home page	www.netscape.com	Online help
New SAT	www.collegeboard.com/student/testing/newsat/about.html	Preview of the New SAT
New School Online University	www.dialnsa.edu	Online undergrad degree offered by New School
New York Times' Education Coverage	www.nytimes.com/pages/education.html	Information about colleges in NY and elsewhere
Newbies Anonymous: A Guide to the Internet	www.geocities.com/TheTropics/1945/index1.htm	An Internet introduction
News Link	www.newslink.org/statcamp.html	Links to newspapers around the country
Next Stop College	www.collegeboard.com/apply	Online applications
NJCAA Guide for Athletes	www.njcaa.org	Sports programs at Junior Colleges
Office of Postsecondary Education	www.ed.gov/about/offices/list/OPE/index.html	Technical resources from the Dept. of Education
Pacific NW Scholarship Guide	www.collegeplan.org/cpnow/pnwguide/pnwguide.htm	Scholarship-search service for Pacific NW students
Personal Identification Number	www.pin.ed.gov	Apply for a personal identification number
Peterson's Distance Learning	www.petersons.com/distancelearning	Directory of online courses and programs
Peterson's Education Portal	www.petersons.com	Searches, Q-and-A areas, and more
Peterson's Test Prep	www.petersons.com/testprepchannel	Online test prep
Pick-a-Prof	www.pick-a-prof.com	Faculty evaluations
Plagiarism.org	www.plagiarism.org	Site to help professors catch online plagiarists
PLATO	www.plato.org	Source for private loans
PNC Bank	www.eduloans.pncbank.com	Source for federal student loans
Prepstar	prepstar.com	Recruiting service
Presidential Freedom Scholars	www.nationalservice.org/scholarships	Information on Presidential Freedom Awards
Princeton Review's 351 Best Colleges	www.princetonreview.com/college/research	Colleges ranked by students

Name	Address (URLs, etc.)	What's inside
Princeton Review's Counselor-O-Matic	www.princetonreview.com/college/research	Database of college descriptions
Princeton Review's Forums	discuss.princetonreview.com	Online discussions about choosing a college
Princeton Review's Interview Advice	www.princetonreview.com/college	Interview advice
Princeton Review's Test Prep	www.princetonreview.com/college/testPrep	Online test prep
Professional and Graduate Schools	www.gradschools.com/search.html	Links to home pages of graduate schools
PROFILE	profileonline.collegeboard.com	PROFILE Registration and Q-and-A
Quicken	www.quicken.com	Investment advice
Roomate Service.com	www.roommates.com	Roommate matching service
ROTC Headquarters	www.defenselink.mil/faq/pis/19.html	Information on ROTC
Sage Tuition Rewards Program	www.student-aid.com	Investment program for parents
Sallie Mae	www.salliemae.com	Information on loans and the company itself
SAT Dates	www.collegeboard.com/student/testing/sat/calenfees.html	Standardized testing information
SAT Registration	www.collegeboard.com/testing	Standardized testing information
Scholarship Research Network	www.smexpress.com	Scholarship-search service
Scholarship Scams	www.ftc.gov/bcp/conline/edcams/scholarship	Tips on spotting scams
ScholarStuff	www.scholarstuff.com	Searches, Q-and-A areas, and more
Scout USA	www.scoutusa.com	Recruiting service
Search	www.search.com	Metasearch engine
Secondary School Report Form	www.nacac.com/downloads.html	For guidance counselors
Security on Campus, Inc.	www.campussafety.org	Information about crime on campus
Servicemembers Opportunity College	www.soc.aascu.org	Online degrees for servicemembers and their families
SmartMoney Magazine	www.smartmoney.com/college	Investing for college
Soc.college	Soc.college	Q-and-A bulletin board
Soc.college.admissions	Soc.college.admissions	Q-and-A bulletin board
Soc.college.financial-aid	Soc.college.financial-aid	Advice and commiseration
Southern California Schools and Colleges	www.latimes.com/news/learning	Information about colleges in Southern California
Southern Regional Electronic Campus	www.electroniccampus.org	Online education at southern universities
Southwest Student Services	www.sssc.com	Source for federal student loans
State Education Agencies	bcol02.ed.gov/Programs/EROD/org_list.cfm	Links to state-specific sites on financial aid
State Guaranty Agencies	bcol02.ed.gov/Programs/EROD/org_list.cfm	List of state loan guaranty agencies
State Higher-Education Agencies	bcol02.ed.gov/Programs/EROD/org_list.cfm	Links to state-specific sites on financial aid
Student Counseling Virtual Pamphlet Collection	counseling.uchicago.edu/vpc/virtulets.html	Links to virtual pamphlets on counseling topics

Name	Address (URLs, etc.)	What's inside
Student Doctor Network	www.studentdoctor.net	Searches, Articles, Advice and more for Pre-meds
Student Guide	www.studentaid.ed.gov/guide	The government's guide to federal student aid
Student Loan Funding	www.studentloanfunding.org	Source for federal student loans
Student.Com	www.student.com	Articles, chat rooms, and links to college life sites
StudentAdvantage.Com	www.studentadvantage.com	Discounts, articles, tools
Studentjobs.gov	www.studentjobs.gov/d_coop.asp	Cooperative Education with the Federal Government
Student MVP	studentmvp.com	Recruiting service
Students.Gov	www.students.gov	Department of Education's central student aid site
Study Hall	www.studyhall.com	Online test prep
Studyabroad.com	www.studyabroad.com	Browsable information on study-abroad programs
SunTrust Bank	www.suntrusteducation.com	Source for federal student loans
SUNY Learning Network	sln.suny.edu	Online education at State University of NY schools
Teoma	www.teoma.com	Search engine and catalog of the Web
TestU	www.testu.com	Free, online prep"
Texas Guaranteed Student Loan Corporation	www.AdventuresinEducation.org	About paying for college
Texas Guaranteed Student Loan Corporation	www.tgslc.org	About paying for college
The Education Research Institute	www.teri.org	Source for private loans
The List	www.thelist.com	List of Internet Service Providers
The Slot	www.theslot.com	Online style manual
The Street	www.thestreet.com	Investment advice
Thesaurus	www.thesaurus.com	Online version of Roget's Thesaurus
Tuition Management Systems	www.afford.com	Administers monthly-payment plans
TuitionPay from Academic Management Service	www.tuitionpay.com	Administers monthly-payment plans
Turn It In	www.turnitin.com	Site to help professors catch online plagiarists
U.S. News & World Report	www.usnews.com/usnews/ edu/college/cohome.htm	College rankings
U.S. News, Find Your Ideal School	www.usnews.com/usnews/edu/college/tools/brief/cosearch-brief.php	
U.S. News's College Forums	www.usnews.com/usnews/edu/forums.fohome.html	College search
U.S. Universities and Community Colleges	www.utexas.edu/world/univ	The most vexing questions
United Negro College Fund	www.uncf.org	Links to home pages of colleges in the U.S.
Universal Black Pages	www.ubp.com	Scholarships typically for minority students
University of Phoenix	www.phoenix.edu	Articles and links to sites about HBCUs
UPromise	www.upromise.com	Online business education
		Investment program for parents

Name	Address (URLs, etc.)	What's inside
US Bank	www.usbank.com/studentloans	Source for federal student loans
U-Wire	www.uwire.com	Links to top stories from student newspapers
Vanguard	www.vanguard.com	Investment advice
Varsity Books	www.varsitybooks.com	Online source for college textbooks
Virtual University Gazette	www.geteducated.com/vugaz.htm	Electronic newsletter on distance education
Washington CollegePost	washingtonpost.com/wp-dyn/education/highereducation	Information about colleges in Washington, DC
Wells Fargo	wellsfargo.com/per/accounts/student	Source for federal student loans
Western Governors University	www.wgu.edu	Virtual university
WiredScholar (from Sallie Mae)	www.wiredscholar.com	Searches, Q-and-A areas, and more
Women's College Coalition	www.womenscolleges.org	Links to home pages of women's colleges
Women's Sports Foundation	www.womenssportsfoundation.org	Sports information for women
Wordsmyth Educational Dictionary-Thesaurus	www.wordsmyth.net	Online dictionary
Wordsmyth S.A.T. Dictionary	www.lightlink.com/bobp/wedt/sat.htm	Dictionary of words that appear on SAT
World Alumni Net	www.Alumni.net	Direct links to college alums
World Wide Learn	www.worldwidelearn.com	Directory of online courses and programs
Writing the College Admission Essay	icpac.indiana.edu/publications/infoseries/is-15.html	Advice on writing college essays
XAP Applications	www.xap.com/apply	Online applications
XAP's Mentor Web Sites	www.xap.com/gotocollege	Database of college descriptions
Yahoo!	www.yahoo.com	Search engine and catalog of the Web
Yahoo's list of e-zines	dir.yahoo.com/News_and_Media/College_and_University/Magazines	Links to more college-life magazines
Yahoo's College Listings-United States	dir.yahoo.com/Education/Higher_Education/Colleges_and_Universities	Links to home pages of colleges in the U.S.
Yahoo's List of Distance Education Options	dir.yahoo.com/Education/Distance_Learning	List of distance education sites
Yahoo's List of Lenders	dir.yahoo.com/Education/Financial_Aid/Loans	Links to sites maintained by lenders
Yahoo's Overview of Distance Education	degrees.education.yahoo.com	Overview of distance education opportunities
Your Virtual Interview	www.bergen.org/AAST/Projects/CollegePrep/Interview.html	Virtual Interview Practice
YourNotes	www.yournotes.com	Online class notes for UPenn
ZipLip.com	www.ziplip.com	Private e-mail accounts
ZixMail	www.zixmail.com	Privacy enhancements to existing email

College Planning Guides from Octameron

Don't Miss Out: The Ambitious Student's Guide to Financial Aid **$12.00**
Hailed as the top consumer guide to student aid, *Don't Miss Out* covers scholarships, loans, and personal finance strategies. It will save readers hundreds, if not thousands of dollars in college costs.

The A's and B's of Academic Scholarships **$10.00**
Money for being bright! This book describes 100,000 awards offered by nearly 1200 colleges. Best of all, most of these (which must be used at the sponsoring school) are not based on financial need.

Loans and Grants from Uncle Sam **$8.00**
Increase your eligibility for federal student aid. This guide describes it all—the aid application process as well as loans and grants for students, parents and health professionals.

SAT Savvy: Last Minute Tips and Strategies **$10.00**
Nervous about the SAT? Whether you took a test prep course or are relying on innate ability, SAT Savvy contains all the tips you need to boost your confidence and your scores.

Majoring in Success: Building Your Career While Still in College **$8.00**
Take advantage of internships, work-study, volunteerism and cooperative education to offset college costs, connect with future employers, build a strong resume, prepare for job interviews, and much more.

Financial Aid Officers: What They Do—To You and For You **$5.00**
Should you accept your award package as offered? Can you request it be changed, or increased? Knowledgeable dealings with FAOs can result in more money. This book shows you how.

Behind the Scenes: An Inside Look at the College Admission Process **$7.00**
Ed Wall, former Dean of Admission at Amherst College, offers sage advice and detailed profiles of successful applicants. An invaluable view from inside on how the selection process really works.

Do It Write: How to Prepare a Great College Application **$6.00**
Personalize your essays so they stand out from the crowd. Author Gary Ripple is the former Ad

College ... **$10.00**
Auth
advice t

Campu **$5.00**
Nerv
advice t

Colleg . **$10.00**
Lost
financi

Camp ... **$7.00**
Lea
Author

Finan ... **$8.00**
Lea

The W ... **$7.00**
It's
athletic

Colle ... **$7.00**
Incl

Colle . **$10.00**
Get
college
lifesty!

Calcu . **$45.00**
Esti
softwa

Ord
Sen
703-8
Please
Meth
Maste